Confessions of a Pastor's Wife

Crossroads Lead to
Life's Purpose

by

Sharon Lebsack

Confessions

of a

Pastor's Wife

Crossroads Lead to

Life's Purpose

by

Sharon Lebsack

Copyright © 2017 Sharon Lebsack
All rights reserved.
ISBN: ISBN-13: 978-1973835066
ISBN-10: 1973835061

This non-fiction work is based on true events. However, some names of people and/or places have been changed to protect those involved.

The works of guest pastors' wives were used with permission and belonged to each author individually.

Bold font on Scripture quotations has been added by the author for emphasis.

THE HOLY BIBLE, NEW INTERNATIONAL VERSION®, NIV® Copyright © 1973, 1978, 1984, 2011 by Biblica, Inc.®. Used by permission. All rights reserved worldwide.

Scripture quotations from The Authorized (King James) Version. Rights in the Authorized Version in the United Kingdom are vested in the Crown. Reproduced by permission of the Crown's patentee, Cambridge University Press

The ESV® Bible (The Holy Bible, English Standard Version®). ESV® Permanent Text Edition® (2016). Copyright © 2001 by Crossway, a publishing ministry of Good News Publishers. The ESV® text has been reproduced in cooperation with and by permission of Good News Publishers. Unauthorized reproduction of this publication is prohibited. All rights reserved.

Partner with SycamoreTreePress.com

It's good to be Zacchaeus and have Jesus to your house for tea,
It's better to be the Sycamore tree and lift others up to see.

WHAT PEOPLE ARE SAYING ABOUT
Confessions of a Pastor's Wife

"In this book, Sharon identifies herself as the wife of a pastor and tells her story with unusual transparency. This story includes fascinating anecdotes, faith-demanding challenges, difficult valleys, and great victories. All who read this story, including women who serve in a similar role, will find purpose, inspiration, practical guidance, and spiritual direction. My wife, Esther, and I attended the church where Lee and Sharon served as pastors. To us Sharon was an ideal pastor's wife and an outstanding role model for others." ~George Flattery

George M. Flattery, Ed.D. is Chancellor, Global University Founder, Network211, and authored: *"The Paradox of Leadership", "Becoming Great through Service", "A Systematic Approach to a Vibrant Relationship"*, and more.

"You'll strike up a friendship with Sharon as you relive her stories. Be prepared to nod in agreement, giggle and cringe as you encounter the nuances of life in the fast lane of ministry. You'll come to know the heart and intent of the author as you read the real-life experiences of a ministry family. It's a fun read that packs truth and purpose into the suitcase of reality." ~Judy Rachels

Judy Rachels is a lifelong woman in ministry. District Women's Ministry Director. National Director of Network of Women's Ministers. Sought after speaker.

Confessions of a Pastor's Wife is the real, raw and rare look behind the scenes of the trials and triumphs of a woman and her family walking out obedience to God. You will laugh and you will cry. You will realize that life is not easy, even for a preacher's wife, But God is good all the time. ~Kendall Bridges

Kendall Bridges – is Lead Pastor at Freedom Church and author, of *Better Marriage - Against All Odds*.

DEDICATION

To you, my friends, who never gave up on finding God's purpose for your life.

For those of you who have chosen to put rejection, criticism, self-pity, and your family in God's hands.

To you who never gave into the power of your position as the "pastor's wife."

This book can produce fruit in your life and be your future testimony—a guide to finding your purpose, to foster your love for Jesus, others, and yourself.

ACKNOWLEDGMENTS AND THANKS

To God: I thank You and acknowledge the One who created me, had a plan for my life and never gave up on me.

To my husband, Lee: Thank you for believing I could do anything. During these 58 years of our life together, you encouraged me, held me, and let me cry when I was overwhelmed. You listened to me read aloud story after story of our life as I wrote this book. You encouraged me to continue on this book-writing journey. You've always loved me unconditionally. I love it when you call me "Sweetheart," and "Miss America." I love you.

To our three daughters and sons-in-law—Tami and John, Tonya and Mark, Tiffany and Vince: There are no words to tell you how much you are loved, cherished and admired. Each one of you has encouraged me in some way to write this account of my life. Thank you for your inspiration, helping to make decisions, ideas, and suggestions as I wrote this book. You will never know how you have contributed to my life and how much I love you. I am blessed beyond words.

To our grandchildren: Krystal and Justin, Caleb, Kayla and Brett, Justin and Tara, Jackson and Avery. This love is like no other. You've brought such joy to my life with your smiles, hugs, words of love, and concern. If I feel lonely, homesick or down, I will call or Facetime you and that turns my sad face into a smile every time. Thank you for the excitement you've shared about your Mama Kay (my grandma name) writing a book. I love it!

To our great-grandchildren: Brynley, Haven, Lyla, and Cole. What a thrill to hold you, love you and watch you grow. You are the fourth generation of precious little ones to our family. Thank you for the joy you bring to my heart.

To my friends: thank you for your opinions and advice when I was in the middle of making major decisions. For those of you who helped with suggestions, ideas, and editing: Barbara, Fluffy, Jill, and Martha.

To Caleb: Thank you for encouraging me to stay with the title I had from the beginning, 25 years ago, "The Confessions of a Pastor's Wife." Then you came up with the idea for the sub-title: "Crossroads that Lead to Life's Purpose." I'm waiting for you to write your book.

To Frankie Cardinal (Caleb's fiancée): thank you for the sketches you drew for sections of my book. You are gifted, talented and loved.

To Anita Watson for also contributing to sketches in my book.

To the pastors' wives: You are my friends who were willing to share your heart with experiences of your own. I give you a "high five" for being vulnerable and brave in telling your stories. Thank you for your friendship, love, and camaraderie.

To Linda Throop: Thank you for helping me to get started from the very beginning. I had notes, journals, bible verses underlined, but nothing on the computer. You gave me direction and encouragement that my unorganized story could actually become a book.

To Peggy Purser Freeman, the editor I've chosen to take

me to the completion of my book: Your talents and gifts were what I needed. Thank you for understanding me and keeping my personality throughout the book.

To Stevo Flores from Righteous Creative: Thank you for the beautiful photography for the cover of "Confessions of a Pastor's Wife." You brought to life my ideas and suggestions. You're good!

Content

	Acknowledgments	ix
	Introduction	15
	Part One – The Journey Begins	17
1	Divine Grace	19
2	The Road to Emmaus in a 1959 Impala	27
3	Boot Camp	31
4	Motel Blessings	39
	Part Two - A Church, Children, and Other Miracles	43
5	God Turned for Good	45
6	Encouragement	51
7	Ravenna, Ohio	53
8	God's Bonus	65
9	A Bend in the Dream	79
	Part Three - South Bend, Indiana	**85**
10	Around the Bend	87
11	A Bend in the Road	**95**
12	Bend the Rules	**107**
13	Love Unbending	**123**
	Part Four - Dallas, Texas	**137**
14	Destination Dallas	**139**
15	Real Friend or NOT	151

16	When the Cat's Away the Mice Play	157
	Part Five - Retirement	**169**
17	No Longer a Pastor's Wife	171
18	Being Ministered To	185
19	Paradise Found	193
	Part Six - Other Pastors' Wives	201
20	Tami	203
21	Joy	207
22	Judy	**211**
23	Darla	215
24	Kate	219
25	Roberta	223
26	Shannon	227
	Part Seven - Looking Foreword	231
27	Sharon's True Confessions	233
	About the Author	**236**

Introduction

I married a minister when I had little knowledge of what my life would be. Fifty-eight years later, I look back down the road traveled knowing God has always been in the driver's seat. He knew where I was going. It's my hope that as you read this book, you feel encouraged in your ministry and your faith. I pray that my story will shine a light on the pastor's co-worker (his wife) and give all those who minister a new hope.

We strive to be the Proverbs 31 woman, to emulate her values and virtues. There's no magic formula to erase the bad. However, I wanted to share how I got through fifty years of ministry without becoming bitter and still hold on to a spirit of thankfulness for the good, the bad, and the ugly that the Father has carried me through, for in the journey I have been blessed.

Before I formed you in the womb I knew you, before you were born I set you apart. Jeremiah 1:5 [NIV]

My story is unique just as yours. I wouldn't want to trade places with you and you wouldn't want to trade places with me.

I encourage you to embrace your life, your circumstances, and your story. God's plan and purpose for your journey are that you:

Accept who you are.
Accept where you are.
Accept where you've been.

Sharon Lebsack

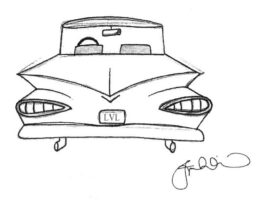

Part One
The Journey Begins

The Journey is where the process takes place—the process of becoming the person God intended us to be.

In the first five years of our ministry, my husband Lee and I traveled. Most of the time we stayed in other people's homes and wrapped our schedule into their family's life. It wasn't what I signed up for—but God had other plans. This is where my ministry life began. In spite of the fact that I dislike this part of my personal timeline, I begin here because it reflects the blessings God has for women who follow Him in ministry.

Sharon Lebsack

Chapter 1
Divine Grace

How is it, Lord, that men and women look at things so differently?
~ Sharon Lebsack

Dead! I'm dead. I bolted up from a deep sleep, blinked away a bad dream, and shivered from a cold sweat. The feeling of having been anesthetized hovered over me. I stumbled out of bed and paced around the room. *Had I died and gone to heaven?* Hopefully, it was heaven. In my mind, I knew I was walking around in my parent's guest bedroom, but I felt dead—zombie-like or at least drugged and unfeeling. I couldn't speak, and so I left my husband sleeping.

What is this, Lord?

In all my life, I had never felt such a powerful experience. When my breathing grew steady, my mind focused on the present. This is ridiculous! If I was in heaven, it certainly wouldn't look like my parent's guest bedroom.

I walked to our family room and sat on the couch trying to cautiously figure out why this strange phenomenon was happening. All I could do was pray.

Jesus, I know you are here for me. But, God, what is this?

Sharon Lebsack

How in the world did I get here, in this place, this time, and facing this dramatic change of my comfortable lifestyle? This was the day that my life would change forever. Lee and I were starting out in full-time ministry. God was evidently allowing me this time to reflect on how I got to this place and this time.

I shook my head to clear the nightmare and allowed my memories to take me back to where all of this started, God's divine grace in review.

Memories flowed over me—high school graduation, my life while attending Evangel University, and meeting my future husband, Lee Lebsack. The memories flooded over me. The decision to switch from attending Ohio State University to Evangel University in midsummer was a big move on my part. I had tried to explain switching universities to my father.

"No, Dad, I don't want to be a preacher. I just want to know more about the Bible!" As my parents dropped me off to officially be on my own, I could see the confusion on my dad's face.

I loved being on my own and making new friends. I soon realized most of the men were there because of a call to ministry in their lives. Then I met Lee. He played on the all-star basketball team and in the band. He had many friends and conveyed an attitude of knowing where he was going in life. I was drawn to his good looks, athletic abilities, music abilities, and self-confidence. As we dated, I found myself falling in love with a man who was called to be a pastor. I was young and had no concept of what it was like to be a minister's wife.

We dated a year and were engaged for another year. I didn't believe I had a call to be a pastor's wife, only to know more about studying God's word. However, during these two years reality set in of what might be ahead.

My dream for life, as I saw it, was to be a supportive wife and mother, thinking whatever profession my husband had, I could fulfill that role. After all, this was what I had experienced as a child. My mother was a loving, supporting wife of my dad who was a GM executive. She gave everything for her children in caring, loving, teaching, and training. I could do that. *Was that what I wanted for my future?*

I knew nothing of the life of a pastor's wife as I had only seen my pastor's wife once a week for a couple of hours. She seemed so in control of everything in life. How did she do it? Maybe I could do that—have a church family to support and love me as I grow into the role.

Well into our year of engagement, Lee shared with me his plan of furthering his education by holding meetings as a traveling evangelist. This would put him in direct contact with pastors to discover more about how to grow a church, deal with issues, troubled people, staff relations, and much more. Preaching every night would give him the opportunity to write sermons and interact with the congregation.

Wait a minute! Traveling? An evangelist! I had just worked through the process of being a pastor's wife. Now, this? This could definitely be a deal-breaker. I had real doubts if I could in any way be a part of this traveling evangelist's life. As I sought God for answers, He assured me this was His plan for my life.

One of the scriptures that helped me through that decision comforted me again as a young bride, sitting in my parents' living room in the middle of the night. I slowly got up from the couch, pinching myself to see if I was alive, awake, and aware of what was taking place right now. Evidently, in starting this new journey, I still wasn't sure if it had been a dream or nightmare. But God had a plan and purpose for my life.

(Sharon,) be careful to do what the Lord your God has commanded you, do not turn aside to the right or to the left. Deuteronomy 5:32 [NIV]

Now, I'm a grown-up married woman sitting in my parents' living room, and my fears rush to the surface like oil in water. I wasn't what I used to be, or who I wanted to be. I wasn't the perfect godly woman Lee would need. I felt frozen. But, I am a child of God in training. My old life faded as I pressed on toward something new—something out of a movie—God's movie.

(Yes, Sharon,) know what I am commanding you today is not too difficult for you or beyond your reach. Deuteronomy 30:11 [NIV]

It had only been a little over a year since Lee and I said, "I do." The ceremony took place in my home church, Bethel Temple in Dayton, Ohio. I have trusted God and I trust this man who I promised to follow into a new zone. Love from God and love from Lee was all I need to begin this journey.

I went back to bed and slept soundly until the alarm startled me out of sleep once again. This time when I walked around that room, I felt alive, not dead—focused, not fearful. Getting up this morning, having coffee, taking a shower, dressing, and putting final items in our suitcase was beyond real—it was surreal. Lee waited impatiently for me as I moved slowly, trying to process the day. Lee had been waiting for this day since entering college as a teenager. I might have been dragging my feet, but continued—ready, willing, and able.

As we prepared to leave, I thought of the wedding gifts we were leaving behind. All the beautiful things of my dream wedding waited to decorate our happy-ever-after. My heart sank.

"I can't believe we have to leave all the beautiful gifts in my parents' attic."

"Sharon," Lee took my shoulders, turned me toward him. "You will love traveling. No cooking or cleaning, just singing every night, seeing souls find Christ, and meeting new people every two weeks." Lee saw an adventure. I saw a dream disrupted. *How is it, Lord, that men and women look at things so differently?*

"But I love to clean and cook. I don't know if I will like meeting new people every two weeks, not to mention living with strangers."

Lee continued trying to convince me, "But, Sharon, we will be staying with pastors—godly men—and you will love traveling." One of the things that attracted me to Lee was his strong personality. He knew what he wanted and worked diligently until his plan was accomplished.

"But, God?" I whispered. Then He reminded me that I had already prayed through on this topic. Finally, God's Spirit released me from fear and doubt with this scripture:

He hath not given me the spirit of fear, but power, love, and a sound mind. 2 Timothy 1:7 [KJV]

I surely needed that—power, love, and a sound mind.

A verse in Deuteronomy became an answer to me then and again now.

Sharon Lebsack

(Sharon,) **Be careful to do what the Lord your God has commanded you; do not turn aside to the right or to the left. Walk in all the way that the Lord your God has commanded you, so that you may live and prosper and prolong your days in the land that you will possess. Deuteronomy 5:32-33 [NIV]**

Both sets of our parents presented us with a blue and white, 1959 Chevrolet Impala as a wedding gift. The make of the car was quite important to me because my father worked as a General Motors (GM) executive. I had been taught from a very young age that GM cars were the only good cars made. While in college, I even sorrowfully called my father with the very disturbing news that Lee's father drove a Ford. This could be a deal-breaker. Regretfully, his father was also of the opposite political party that I had been led to believe was unerring. I was almost in tears when my calm, composed father told me he appreciated my loyalty, but a Ford was no doubt just as absolute as a GM Chevrolet. A marriage in ministry travels down many bumpy roads. Cars and politics weren't the only differences in our marriage.

My parents walked us out to our car. We hugged with final words of goodbye until Christmas. I tried to pretend that this was just like any other time, knowing down deep it wasn't. This was a profoundly emotional time in my life. My father's clear blue, loving eyes reflected the concern that he shared with my mother years ago.

"I am very anxious," my father had said, "that Sharon will have a hard time making it in life because of her timidity and lack of confidence."

I have always been out to do whatever to prove that

statement wrong. It became a challenge and necessary motivation for me to do more than enough. I'm getting a chance now. I never dreamed my destiny for life would be this enormous. I wasn't disheartened over his evaluation of my character. It just became a way of life for me—striving to turn a weakness into a strength.

As he stood with his arm around my mother, watching me leave, he no doubt was thinking those exact words now. My father was a good man, but not a believer at this time.

"Will she make it in life?" No doubt, he thought I might be out of my mind. *But, God?*

We got in the car and my soul whispered, *Here we go!* It matters not who we are, God knows us by name and He has prepared us for such a time as this.

(Sharon,) **Before I formed you in the womb, I knew you, before you were born I set you apart. Jeremiah 1:5 [NIV]**

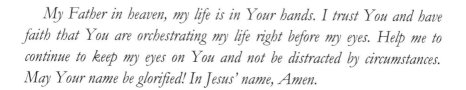

My Father in heaven, my life is in Your hands. I trust You and have faith that You are orchestrating my life right before my eyes. Help me to continue to keep my eyes on You and not be distracted by circumstances. May Your name be glorified! In Jesus' name, Amen.

Sharon Lebsack

Chapter 2
The Road to Emmaus in a 1959 Impala

"Stay calm and drive a Chevy!" ~Dad

As we said goodbye to my parents, a lump grew in my throat. We wouldn't see them for six months, not until Christmas. We sped into the future in a car filled with suitcases, musical instruments, including my accordion, and sound equipment. I felt like a sardine in a can with very little room for movement.

Lee booked us in Nebraska, Ohio, Illinois, and Missouri for two-week meetings for one year. Where Lee saw a plan, apprehension clouded my vision. But God had confirmed His plan, and I believed in Lee and trusted him.

As we approached our first revival meeting, I heard Lee saying, "Sharon, are you awake? We are almost there."

"Not sleeping," I said as I jolted out of my deep meditation.

"Yes, I'm ready." I glanced out the windshield and noticed a small church right out of *Little House on the Prairie*. "Yes, hmmm, I think I'm ready. Ready to get off the road for a while. Ready to meet our new friends, see our home—for two weeks."

We pulled up to the small, white church surrounded by beautiful green trees and a few yellow flowers peeking out here and there, for our very first service of this journey. My heart beat a little faster and for a moment I felt almost dizzy. Lee just looked at me with a comforting smile. He took my hand and said, "Let's pray."

Dear Father in Heaven, Hallowed be Thy name. Sharon and I are answering the call which we feel in our hearts. We ask for Your help, direction, and capability to adjust to this new venture of ministry. Thank You, Jesus. Amen.

After the prayer, the strength of God filled us. This was exactly what the doctor ordered for me to pull myself together to meet the pastor and his family. There's always a tinge of excitement for the "unknown," and this was certainly the "unknown" for me. "Okay, let's go," I said.

As we got out of the car and walked to the church, the pastor greeted us with a big smile. "We've been watching for your car. The family can't wait to meet you."

He took us next door to their parsonage. His lovely wife and three elementary-age children showed us to our room. We entered into a shocking pink and yellow room–just Lee's style. The pastor's daughter gave up her room for us and would now be her sister's roommate for the duration of our stay in their home.

As we started unloading the car, the children wanted to help carry things. It was slightly awkward, not having known the people before now, but when we went over to the church to set up our equipment for this first night, excitement sparkled in Lee's eyes and sprang up in my spirit.

Back in our cozy and clean new home, we unpacked, had a few minutes to get used to our room, took a shower, and got dressed. As we rushed to dinner with the family, Lee whispered, "Sharon, I'm not hungry. Are you?"

"No," I replied. "We had that big lunch, but we have to eat. Remember, we are now on their schedule and we can do it. Right?" We both smiled and started downstairs.

A lovely meal filled the table before us, smells of steaming-hot pot roast, freshly baked rolls, and homemade apple pie wafted toward us. We conversed with the family, a bit nervous because we had to quickly get ready for our meeting. When Lee and the pastor went over to the church, I helped clean up the kitchen.

As cars pulled into the parking lot, conflicting emotions engulfed me, both scared and excited at the same time.

Lord, tonight the journey of our lives begins. Bless it.

Little did I realize this schedule would last for five years. I was thinking that this traveling life would no doubt last a couple of years. Then we would have our own home, pastor our own church, and perhaps plan a family. If Lee had said, "This will be our life for the next five years," I don't think I would have done it.

We had chosen the songs and practiced, Lee had prepared his sermons, and church began. We opened with our theme song.

> "Praise the Lord I've been invited to a meeting in the air, Jubilee, Jubilee. All the saints of all the ages, in their glory, will be there, Oh, I'm going to that happy Jubilee."

The congregation joined in the excitement of this song, "Jubilee." We sang and played three songs, and then Lee preached. Lee gave an altar call for people to come and accept Christ. After the service, we met people and prayed for their needs.

During the service, a joy stirred in my heart as Lee and I ministered to the congregation in song. I now knew what it was like to feel the presence of God flood my being. I gave to others what God had done for me. I wanted to be used by God. I had heard of many who sought relief from pain by using drugs, alcohol, and more. I had never felt this high of being an instrument of God before this time. How could I ever have questioned God's direction for my life?

When I would sing "If That Isn't Love," the magnitude of God singing through me brought a joy that I had never known. I soon found out that this would not last forever because "highs" don't last. You need more and more. Assuredly, we had more and more times to give out and we were blessed more than those in the congregation.

Getting home late meant we could sleep in—or maybe not. If we wanted breakfast, we would have to adapt to each family's schedule. Many times people from the congregation would bring food into the parsonage. This worked out well most of the time, and it was nice to have meals prepared for us. Then after two weeks, we packed the car up again. We said, "thank you" and "goodbye" to our new family. Ditto, repeat many times and fast forward five years.

Thank you, Lord Jesus, for showing me I can be a part of this team. This would be my life for the year! Well, okay, Lord. I can do this! Amen.

Chapter 3
Boot Camp

"I will strengthen you." ~God

Each time we left a church and a pastor's family, we took something with us. There were homes where everything was built around the church. The pastor and his family carried church right into their homes, talking about church business. Others who changed from pastors to normal people in their home maintained a balance. They played games and their conversation was built around what was happening within their family. Some ministers and wives seemed quite disturbed, uncomfortable, and stressed over issues in their congregation. They carried the stress into their home and continued their conversation, trying to solve these problems in front of their children.

Some of the wives treated their pastor-husband with the same honor and respect as their doctor, dentist or attorney—the personal attachment void in their relationship. Still, other pastors and their wives showed affection with one another as if they were normal people.

Lee and I spoke of this often and made the decision that we

wanted to be a normal family with a balance of church, family, extracurricular activities, and date nights to keep our marriage strong. We definitely saw how it would take time, effort, and planning to make this happen, but it would be well worth the effort.

As I look back on those five years, I can honestly say this was the "worst of times and the best of times" in my life. Boot Camp–a training time for both of us. Lee would meet with the pastors who mentored him regarding pastoring, shepherding, building a staff, dealing with difficult people, and building and growing a church. He became knowledgeable in performing funerals, dedications, baptisms, and wedding ceremonies.

For me, I saw hands-on what the atmosphere was like in a pastor's home life. I saw many happy pastor's wives, but just as many unhappy, hurting wives and children. This was a learning experience for my future. I had choices of what to do during the day. I didn't want to be in the way of the schedule of the hostess-for-the-week, therefore I stayed in my room most of the time. My mother bought me a sewing machine that gave me something to do. I started making my own clothes. Lee and I practiced songs every day and sometimes drove into the town for a break.

I remember one time after church we were hungry and this particular family didn't eat after church. So we started walking down the street for some quality time together at the Dairy Queen. Soon we heard footsteps behind us and turned to see the pastor and his wife following us. Our special time alone was cut short. Of course, we invited them to have a sundae.

Another time in Nebraska, where a lot of ranchers attended the church, we watched with mouth-watering anticipation as they brought in steaks, roasts, and hamburger. The pastor's wife put it all in the freezer. Next day for dinner, she opened two cans of Campbell's chicken noodle soup. We never had a single meal of beef during our stay. We asked the question, "Where's the beef?"

To this day, we get a chuckle out of a church in Iowa where the congregation brought in so much food, we didn't know what to do with it. There were cakes, pies, salads, casseroles, and more. Wonderful people, the pastor and his wife thanked everyone from the pulpit for their generosity. Well, the food kept coming, so we came up with a phrase when asked if we enjoyed what they brought. We all would just say, "It hit the spot." The spot being the garbage can outside. Laughter became our best friend during these times.

Every Friday night, we had an All Musical Night or a musical production called "Heaven's Gates/Hell's Flames." We wrote the script and used different people as actors. We had a very large framed oilcloth with flames of fire painted on it. The oilcloth represented hell and on the other side of the platform angels in costume represented heaven. We made a realistic professional soundtrack of people screaming and sounds of wailing.

Lee asked me to sing the song, "I Dreamed I Searched Heaven for You." It gave a powerful message to young and old alike.

One night, my parents came to a meeting in Xenia, Ohio. God's Spirit poured down on us. For the first time in his life, my father walked down the aisle to accept Jesus as His Lord and Savior. After all of those years, my mother had been praying for my father, and it finally happened. I was thrilled beyond words.

Tears of joy ran down my cheeks. It was worth everything I had given up and endured for this moment in time.

We kept collecting more "things," packing more instruments, more equipment, more clothes, and props for the play. Our car wasn't just not going to hold anything else. Lee's father called and told us that he and a friend were building us a small trailer to carry our equipment in and a place so we could hang our clothes. We knew we would have plenty of room in the front of the car now. I actually had room for my feet on longer trips.

After a couple of years of this routine, it became pretty normal and I think I had adjusted fairly well to life on the road. We were now ministering in larger churches and the crowds would come for music and preaching. Youth camps invited us to join them in the summer months in Washington State and Ohio, providing a break from the norm and giving us a new desire to reach the youth. We always took the month of August off and either stayed with Lee's parents or mine. We also took most of December off to spend with one or the other. This much needed time of rest blessed us greatly.

At one of the youth camps, an incident occurred which stuck with me for years. We pulled up to the campgrounds, unloaded our car *again*, and located our neatly furnished room. Let's just say, it wasn't the Hilton. Now in this era of the church, girls and boys had different swim times. That was accepted and seemed fine to me. The girl campers' swim time had just been announced. I proceeded to change into my swimsuit. As I ventured out of our cabin, I heard an older woman yelling, "Excuse me. Would you please go back to your room and get your cover-up? Don't you know the rules?"

Embarrassment burned my cheeks as I returned to put on

my cover-up. Then I decided to stop by the location of the "shout out." As I approached the office, I stood face to face with the "old woman." (Old as I saw her because I was still in my early twenties.) I introduced myself as Lee Lebsack's wife. Her face registered total shock. I guess the embarrassment on her face pushed my indignation out of my heart and I let my guard down.

"I am so sorry not to have known the rules," I said softly. It might be better next time to have the rules printed up in the speaker's room."

"My dear," she said and wrapped her arms around me, "I thought you were one of the girls." We both laughed and became good friends.

Although the atmosphere in each place varied, I began to notice a pattern of joy or despair. It was not always talked about, but the parents set the atmosphere of a home.

Some of the pastors would share with Lee their challenges in ministry and some of the wives shared with me some of their struggles in trying to fit into the mold of a pastor's wife. I remember distinctly one pastor's wife who shared her fears for her children entering their teen years.

"What if they wanted to attend school functions when the congregation might believe dances or movies were sinful?" she asked.

Another pastor's wife shared her concern of her daughter who would have to come in late to Youth Night because of drama practice. The fear was always, "What will the church think and my husband could possibly lose his job over something like this."

One concern was a son playing on the basketball team. Practice was on Wednesday night during church. The boy's father was the pastor and told his son he had to leave practice early to make it to church on time. The son felt apprehensive over this. Every time he had to leave, the coach. sarcastically snarled, "So, son, you have to go to *prayer meeting,*?"

We saw joy, happiness, fulfillment, but also pain, depression, and sadness. It didn't take long until God laid a real burden upon my heart for the dear women I met. Little did I know that this again was God's way of preparing me for a future with "Women in Ministry."

Lee and I talked about the different situations. We learned so much by living in the ministers' homes. Lee and I discussed the different family connections and quickly came to the conclusion that balance was our goal. We wanted our children to love God, the church, and the congregation, but knew there was life outside of this life. We decided that we would make the decisions for our family, not a church. We would set the rules. After all, it's our right as parents. We wanted to train up our children in the way they should go and that foundation would be firm. We also made the decision not to discuss any church problems or people in front of our children. They were young and very vulnerable to words, actions, and deeds. Of course, we knew we would not have perfect children because there are none and neither Lee nor I were perfect—then, now, or ever.

One day I sat in our room sewing when I needed a pair of scissors. I went down to ask the pastor's wife to borrow a pair. She went to a drawer and handed them to me. She seemed a quiet, introverted, and sad person. After using the scissors, I put them back in the drawer.

At dinner that night she accused me of not returning her scissors. She demanded that I return them to her. This was awkward.

I wanted to yell. *Are you accusing me of stealing?* Anger, hurt, and sadness whirled within me. I answered as calmly as I could, "I put them back in the drawer after I used them." As a Christian and a minister's wife, I had to forgive her, but I will never forget how this woman took her frustrations out on me. This became another lesson in forgiveness, understanding, and ignoring bad behavior in others, all while being a pastor's wife. God knows what He is doing in these training times.

So much of the time, the minister's wives took me under their wing as a mentor would. After all, I was young and so naive about this journey.

I appreciated the times some of the pastors' wives would encourage me on the sacrifice of not having my own home. "It will come soon enough," one woman shared. "This is your time of learning and understanding."

Others shared techniques of getting along with people by not judging. They showed me how important forgiveness and acceptance is in relationships with church members. Their encouragement helped me understand others. If people could see Jesus in me, that would be the best testimony I could give. I always appreciated their encouragement to just be myself without offending others. I saw firsthand how so many presented Jesus in their words, actions, and deeds. One of the best pieces of advice was to try and realize that those who would criticize and cause dissension had challenges and problems of their own. By putting others down, they were trying to make themselves feel better. The encouragement the wives gave was the confidence they received on their journey. The families who seemed to be the most stable, loving, kind, and functional all lived in agreement with putting their family first.

This became a great lesson to learn. However, it didn't come easy or naturally.

1. Trying to please people would end upside down.
2. Fear of being judged, criticized or gossiped about brings disappointment, anger, frustration, and much more.

When anxiety was great within me, your consolation brought me joy. Psalm 94:19 [NIV]

The Lord is my light and my salvation, whom shall I fear? The Lord is the stronghold of my life, of whom shall I be afraid? Psalm 27:1 [NIV]

Father, I thank You for Your word that is a lamp for my feet and a light for my path. May I always follow Your way, Your path, and Your light. Amen.

Chapter 4
Motel Blessings

Open eyes see the total picture. ~Sharon Lebsack

Holding meetings in larger churches meant hotels, motels or apartments. Oh, how we loved the privacy! Of course, some of the places were downright dirty. I would scrub them down with bleach before unpacking. A church in Wichita, Kansas, owned an apartment building and a unit became available. Excitement washed over both of us. It looked clean, nice, and private.

We unpacked our clothes for the two-week stay. I would get to cook and clean. We even had a closet and drawers. A real home! After retiring the first night, I awoke to the feel of something crawling on my leg. I sat straight up in bed and called out to Lee, who was sound asleep. He got up and turned on the light. I threw down the covers and cockroaches scampered out.

I screamed, "Hurry! Get all of our clothes out of the closet back in our trailer."

"We—we will have to move out of this apartment," Lee stammered.

I answered, "I'm not moving out of this apartment. We can finally have some alone time. We will get cans of bug killer and spray around our bed every night."

The next morning Lee shared with the pastor about our incident and he graciously offered for us to move in with his family, but Lee told him our plan and he understood. *Thank you, Lord, for bug spray!* We never saw another cockroach.

You never think about getting sick when you're doing God's work, but one day the flu hit the town where we ministered. It happened to be on a Friday night, our All Musical Night. We took care of ourselves all day, but could not cancel the program. We saw the crowds coming in; it would be a packed house. We got dressed and took our bottle of Kaopectate. Things were moving along quite well when Lee rushed off of the platform. I stepped up with a testimony until he came back. When flu symptoms hit, it's a Kaopectate event. After a couple more songs, my turn to scoot off the platform occurred. We made it through the program that night, went home, and slept all the next day. God is good!

By this time we considered starting a family, but questions outnumbered answers. Could we have a child without a permanent home? I really was ready for a baby and I would have all the time in the world to take care of a little one. But how could we solve all the challenges of travel?

Then one day God sent the answer. We were expecting. The main problem in pregnancy was I had to go to a different doctor every month. One blessing—I wasn't sick a day. I even had enough room around my tummy area to continue playing my accordion until I was eight months pregnant. Thank God, in the final month we stayed with my parents until our little one was born.

Tamre Kay (Tami) joined the musical Lebsack team on August 24, 1964, in Dayton, Ohio. She was a healthy and good baby girl. Tami filled a void in my life and brought fulfillment at a time I so needed it. For once, I felt purpose in *my* life. No longer just a pastor's wife, I was now a mom.

We had been traveling for almost four years now and my heart longed for our own home. I felt I had enough training on being a pastor's wife. I still felt the joy of ministering at night, but during the day, my life felt useless. Bored sometimes, sad sometimes, I wished for my own home where I could cook, clean, and raise my children. My mind would take me to places I did not want to go—questions warring inside.

What if this is what you will be doing the rest of your life? No, no, I want to unpack my wedding gifts and decorate my house with things I like, sleep in the same bed every night, throw suitcases away, and perhaps have friendships.

Now, Tami brought something wonderful to fill my time 24/7. When she was five weeks old, we piled Tami, all of our equipment, plus a dresser, high chair, potty chair, walker, stroller, and much more into our trailer and started out. *(Note: This was before disposable diapers.)* We made her a bed in the back seat of our car, where she slept well. (Note: This was before car seats were mandatory.) The new journey took on a divine excitement.

Tami never missed a night of services. I would select a member of the congregation to be her nanny and no one else was to hold her.

At the age of one, Tami developed chronic bladder infections. Our challenge was to stop the infection in time. It was very painful for this child. Remember, we moved every two weeks, so when she needed a doctor, it was always someone new. This affliction continued and I struggled with this dilemma.

Lord, we are sacrificing on this journey in obedience to You, so why?

I pleaded for God to give it to me instead, but He had other plans. For a period of about six months, Lee felt a tug at his heart to change ministries and move to being a lead pastor. We had five very productive, challenging years of traveling from east to west, north to south. and God had a plan laid in place for us. Trusting and waiting on Him, we prayed.

The answer may not always look like a picture of the scenic Colorado Rockies, Mount Rushmore, moonlight on the Atlantic Ocean, or even a beautiful sunset in Hawaii, but the answer is there or on its way. Don't miss the answer. Accept God's plan and give thanks.

Our dear God in Heaven, How immature and selfish I have been in the beautiful plan that You laid out for me. Please forgive me for the times I complained, cried, and soaked in self-pity. My eyes are often blinded to Your plan for teaching and training. Open my eyes that I might see. Amen.

Part Two
A Church, Children, and Other Miracles

A gentle curve on our God-engineered road led to years of ministry, of pastoring—filling in the gaps where needed—choir director, women's ministry director, youth minister, secretary, and organizing a peaceful home for our family. During these developing years, many disappointments clouded my vision. No doubt this was due to overwork, overachieving, church growth, and relational surprises of Christian people. Satan can step in if he senses exhaustion. Looking back over my timeline, it amazes me to see that everything Satan intended for bad, God turned for my good.

Sharon Lebsack

Chapter 5

God Turned for Good

"Taking time out can be a good thing." ~Sharon Lebsack

After five years of traveling, we contemplated the possibility of taking a pastorate, and we hoped it would be soon. On our first attempt in Nebraska, we followed the protocol the church laid out for new candidates. We traveled to the state for the interview. Lee preached.

Then, before the vote was taken, we were ushered down to the basement to wait. The basement? They said they would come and get us after the vote. The basement—cold, dark, and gloomy—reflected our emotions. There had to be bugs, possibly even snakes, my imagination got out of control. Memories of those cockroaches crawling on me came back like a shooting bullet.

Lee went to the stairs, straining to hear the results of the vote. He turned around, stared at me with a blank look whispering, "We didn't get it!" I had been overcome with happiness as I thought of the luxury of settling down in my own home. Now, the lump in my throat choked me. My dream shattered. We turned to find a quick escape route out of the basement. I had participated in the service with music, smiles, and shaking hands with the board and parishioners. It wasn't just Lee that had been rejected, but me, too. More and more I comprehended my part in the life of a pastor's wife. We were both being hired.

But, God, this? Lee is the one with the call to the church. My call is to my husband. The vote hurt. However, the procedure, the basement, and the public rejection we went through after the vote left scars on my heart.

Lee took off on a hunting trip with his best friend, Jerry, while I went for a long overdue visit with my parents and family. I needed some pampering. While my mother made my favorite foods we caught up on all of the family. I got to spend quality time with my sister, nieces, and nephews, and slowly the scars of rejection disappeared.

Why do we always think God doesn't know what He is doing? He whispers sometimes.

(Listen, Sharon,) "My thoughts are nothing like your thoughts," says the Lord. "And my ways are far beyond anything you could imagine. For just as the heavens are higher than the earth, so my ways are higher than your ways, and my thoughts higher than your thoughts." Isaiah 55: 8-9 [ESV]

How could I forget this powerful proclamation?

After Lee, Tami, and I left our "mini-sabbatical," we fell back into the routine of traveling. In my mind, I lost heart about settling down, thinking perhaps this would be our life for another five years. I guess if I had done it thus far, just maybe I could submit to the call of God for the musical Lebsack team.

"This is not about me, it is about God." When I heard that phrase from a minister, it stuck with me forever and whenever a tidal-wave of self-pity capsized my faith, the phrase rolled me upright once again. *It is about God.*

After a few months of traveling, Lee came into our room. Smiling, he shocked me with his fluctuating tone, "Sharon, what do you think about leaving the evangelistic field to take a pastoral position in Ohio?" My emotions didn't know how to react after that last episode of "church tryout." I inhaled one of my favorite memory verses and exhaled a prayer.

(Sharon,) **Many are the plans in the mind of a man, but it is the purpose of the Lord that will stand. Proverbs 19:21 [ESV]**

"What, when, where, and why?" I gave Lee my full attention.

Lee went on to tell me that he had received a call from the Ohio District Superintendent, asking if he would be interested in coming to Vermilion, Ohio, to pastor a church. Out of my mouth squeaked, "Yes, yes, yes! You did tell him 'yes', didn't you?" Lee assured me that he told Reverend Arthur Parsons that we would be interested, would pray about it, and contact him within a week. We prayed, talked, and agreed. This could be the time for a change in our ministry.

We discovered that the church in Ohio had been started by Reverend Dan Betzer, one of our college friends. This new church, with a new building, had a good beginning—about 100 attendees. This presented an opportunity for us to move into this new position. The timing was right. Tami needed some stability in her life and perhaps a little brother or sister.

Lee was ready to lead this church to the next level. The

church seemed excited about the music we brought from the evangelistic field. We had a church.

It didn't take long for the Vermilion church to outgrow the building. Sunday school classes overflowed into offices, large closets, and anywhere with empty space. There were not a lot of people in this small church to fill volunteer positions. Lee's questions soon began.

"Sharon, do you think you could fill in as my secretary until we can afford a full-time secretary?" Lee asked casually. "Oh, also the women have been asking about starting a Women's Ministry Department, but they have no leader. I know you are already busy, but we really can't afford to hire a Youth Director." I stopped in my tracks and just looked at my husband (my pastor) for a few seconds. Down through the years, I've found if my plate is full with job after job, I felt overwhelmed, depleted, and incapable. I also have found if God is asking, then I change my priorities and it works. God was asking.

Many people found the Lord as their personal Savior in our first church. Our music program had grown. Lee asked if I would start a choir. I was quite apprehensive. However, the years of singing in a radio choir in college gave me confidence and, with God's help, I believed I could do it.

Attaining our goal of reaching our community, we soon felt comfortable. Tami had been an only child for three years. She needed a playmate and we needed one more little one to complete our family. On November 1, 1967, Tonya Rae was born. What a joy this little one was to our family. She was a good baby and life glowed with God's blessings.

"Sharon, I received a call from Reverend Parsons this morning asking if we would be interested in looking at a church in Ravenna, Ohio."

What? I felt a different kind of shock. As I thought of leaving our new church, new home and uprooting so soon, I questioned the suggestion. "Well, how do you feel about this?" I asked.

"You know, Sharon," Lee shared how God had been preparing him for this move, "God never springs things on us without first preparing us for His plan. I've been feeling for a few months that we had led this congregation as far as we could in this building and perhaps another minister could take them to the next level."

This sounded logical to me. Again, I was reminded that I was called to support my husband, not hold him back. "When do we start packing?"

Lee laughed, "At least we were here almost three years and that's better than moving every two weeks."

I raised my eyebrows and nodded my head affirmatively.

If I ever had any doubts about following my husband I was reminded of what God says on the subject of SUBMISSION.

(Sharon,) **But I want you to realize that the head of every man is Christ, and the head of the woman is man, and the head of Christ is God. I Corinthians 11:3 [NIV]**

Jesus lived His entire life in submission to the Father. The Word uses this term "submission" in many places.

Dear Father in Heaven,

I want to thank You for always being there for me. There have been times of adjusting, learning, stretching, and even trying to be obedient when I didn't want to be obedient. Because of Your patience with me and Your plans for me, I trust You. Looking back at the beginning of our traveling ministry, I feel I have been humbled, blessed, and fulfilled. Thank You for the call that You've placed on Lee's life. May the words of my mouth and the thoughts in my mind be acceptable to You, my God and Father. Amen.

Chapter 6

Encouragement

Weakness is a challenge to change! ~Sharon Lebsack

Anytime you're getting ready to make a move, let **Deuteronomy 4** be a reminder for you to consider and take with you on your journey. Our journey is ordered of God on this earth. Because He has called, He will guide. He will give direction because He has called. He will go before you, behind you, and carry you if you grow weary or weak.

1. **Follow the Word.** (Verse 1)
2. **Hold fast!** (Verse 4)
3. **Watch yourself closely. Don't forget who God is and what He has done for you.** (Verse 7)
4. **Teach your children and grandchildren.** (Verse 9)
5. **Listen and remember the Word.** (Verse 10)
6. **Assemble together and teach.** (Verse 10)
7. **Revere the Lord.** (Verse 10b)
8. **Remember the miracles.** (Verse 14)

9. **If you seek the Lord your God, you will find him.** (Verse 29)

10. **When you're in distress, return to God.** (Verse 30)

11. **The Lord is merciful. He will not abandon or destroy you.** (Verse 31)

12. **The Lord is God.** (Verses 32-38)

13. **The Lord God in Heaven keeps his word that it may be well with you and your children.** (Verse 39-40)

Father God, go before me, behind me, and carry me when I grow weary.

Chapter 7

Ravenna, Ohio

"Just love everyone. I'll sort 'em out later." ~God

The decision was made and we found ourselves in the process of moving to Ravenna, Ohio. We were leaving a brand new home—our first to own—and moving into an outmoded home. The parsonage was owned by the church as part of the pastor's financial package. This house needed a lot of work. The congregation in Ravenna painted, cleaned, and made this house look like a beautiful antique home.

From the very first service in Ravenna, Lee brought the excitement of the Lord to this congregation. They had lost hope and waited with anticipation for this new, young pastor, hoping he could bring them new life.

"Sharon," Lee said.

I waited. *Here it comes.*

"We need an adult and youth choir director." He took a breath and continued, "The church needs an overseer for the Women's Ministry Department. Would you be willing to help out here until we can hire staff?"

This, I thought, I could handle. This was a more established church than our last church, with people who had been trained to be leaders in the different ministries.

Holy Ground!

Sunday mornings were often stressful for me. Lee got up early, had his prayer time, got ready, and left for church so he could meet with God and concentrate on his sermon. On the other hand, I had to get the girls and myself ready, get a dinner on, and be prepared to greet people with a "smile!"

One particular Sunday morning the girls were not getting along, plus Tonya didn't want to wear what I had laid out. They had begged me to stay home Sunday night so they could watch "The Wizard of Oz." To this day they think they were abused by not letting them stay home to watch "The Wizard." They knew we never missed church. If the girls were sick, I would take them up to Lee's office, get a teenager from church to stay with them. Then I would be off to direct the choir, greet people, be happy, pray with them, and be in attendance at our services. *We could not miss. What would people think?*

On the way out the door this Sunday morning, one of the girls bumped into a plant and knocked it over, scattering dirt all over our beige carpet. But "the show must go on." Out the door, we scooted. One of the girls cried. Anger washed over me as I tried to pull myself together before entering the church.

Well, Lord, this is just way too hard. I made up my mind when I got to church that day I would not be the "happy pastor's wife." I would just act like I felt—not being hypocritical. As I got the girls out of the car (actually, it was a red pickup truck, not a car, which I drove to church every Sunday morning) I grabbed their hands and hastily lead them in the front door of the church. I put on a stern face. Well, it was already stern. I didn't have to put it on. *Let's just let them see me as I really am on some Sunday mornings. After all, I am just a normal wife and mother. Right? No, not really.* Or so I thought.

The first person who noticed I wasn't smiling and speaking to everyone asked the loaded question, "Is everything okay, Sharon?"

I didn't know what to say because this was all new to me. "Yes, we just had a rough morning." I didn't like the way this felt. I rushed to find a closet or something to go inside alone, to have a come-to-Jesus meeting. I found a door, opened it to a large closet with mops hanging from the wall. A slight, sickening, stench reached my nostrils. But I had trained myself in the years of traveling to ignore much. I went inside, cried and talked to Jesus.

On this particular morning, I was scheduled to sing a solo titled, "We are Standing on Holy Ground," I sniffed. *In this mop closet? Really? Lord, I am not standing on "Holy Ground."*

In spite of me, God did an amazing thing in calming my spirit. Then His amazing grace reached into my heart, assuring me that I was now (in this closet) standing on Holy Ground.

Things didn't go as planned that morning, but God was just the same. I made the choice of my actions, thoughts, and words. Could I get up there and sing that song? Yes, I could, with the help of God. I decided right then and there I wasn't being fake by smiling and speaking to everyone. I just made a choice of how to adjust to my issues. From that time on, I made a choice to make right decisions on how to deal with the unexpected and unplanned situations in my life. Of course, at home, I felt a little more comfortable showing how I felt, but again it was important that I keep that under control too. Every so often I still have to remind myself that I make the choice. Do I choose to stand on Holy Ground or not?

(Sharon,) **Have I not commanded you? Be strong and of good courage; do not be afraid, nor be dismayed, for the LORD your God is with you wherever you go. Joshua 1:9 [NKJV]**

Every Saturday afternoon, one of the dear saints, Sister Snyder, brought three or four desserts for the week. What a treat! I always prepared Sunday's meal before we left for church. To say the least, Sunday was our biggest day of the week. *Wasn't this supposed to be a day of rest? Don't quite get that!* There was Sunday school, the main service, lunch, afternoon break, choir practice, and Sunday night service.

A couple of interesting stories about the girls during this time stir my memory. Tami was almost six and Tonya was two. After dinner and rest time, about 4:00 pm, I took the girls to church with me for adult choir practice, hired babysitters for them and the children of choir members attending practice.

On this night, I taught a new song to the choir. I even remember the name of the song: "Lead Me to That Rock That is Higher Than I." I loved the words that lifted my spirit, along with the powerful musical rendition. Music reaches down into the soul. Our brains actually respond differently to happy and sad music. I loved this hour of teaching, directing, and singing music. It always elevated my spirits to a new level of joy.

"Mrs. Lebsack," the babysitter called through the curtain of music. "Mrs. Lebsack, I think you forgot something in dressing

Tonya." I stepped off the platform to hear the concerned teenage babysitter explaining what happened. Now, Tonya was a very independent child, wanting to do everything by herself and I pretty much let her. She always wanted to dress herself, even wanting to wear a long black wig to daycare. She loved it, so why not? Well, on this day, she dressed herself.

"Mrs. Lebsack, Tonya doesn't have any panties on!"

Oh, my word! How embarrassing. I found Lee in his office and turned this little incident over to him. Then, I went back to the choir, right where I left off.

A few months later, on Sunday during choir practice, one of the choir moms came to me and asked if I knew what some of the older kids were doing while we were having choir practice.

"No, is it something bad?"

"Oh, no," she went on "Your daughter, Tami, started having a class for the six, seven, and eight-year-olds during choir. She teaches a lesson, sings songs, lines them up to go to the restroom, plays games, and sends a note home with one of them each week to bring a snack for the following week."

Surprised and bursting with pride, I couldn't believe it. I didn't know anything about this setup. "Really? How did you find out about this?" The mom told me that her daughter brought home a note to bring cookies for snacks. This mom asked her daughter questions and heard the story of Tami's nursery ministry.

When we got home that night, I approached Tami and Tonya about this class. They both smiled and told me every Sunday afternoon during rest time they studied and planned things for their class. Tonya, of course, was her sister's sidekick and helper. Things like this make a mom and dad so proud. We could foresee real leadership qualities developing.

About this time, the church saw the need for a Mother's Day Out program and felt the little extra income from that program would help with the added expenses of staff and much more. At first, hiring a director and staff was out of the question. The church board officially addressed this plan to me, offering me the position of director. *Who might have recommended me for this position? It was a mystery. Who would know of my teaching certification for elementary school?* We won't mention any names—however, I might be married to him.

My slogan is, "If God is in it, who can stop it? Maybe me, but I won't."

At the interview, I recommended our youth pastor's wife, Avinell, be my co-director. We would be directors, teachers, music, recess, lunch, and "diaper changers." Avinell consented, and we organized an Open House, opening the next day with five children. The first day, one of the children got sick and vomited all over the floor. Avinell and I both looked at each other in unbelief. This wasn't even in our thinking that something of this sort could paralyze us the first day. She got paper towels, a mop, and then proceeded to clean it up. Avinelle gagged while handing me the paper towels and mop.

I took the paper towels and mop, but the closer I got to the mess, my stomach turned upside down. We decided to get Martha, the secretary, to see if she could possibly clean up this disgusting mess, which she did. We might be good teachers, but that was all, janitorial services were not for us.

The school grew and we hired new teachers and staff, which released us from this program. Later, Lee opened a Christian private school (K-7), under the direction of a new staff couple (Mark and Judy Hayburn), who became valuable to our program and great friends. Judy and I really bonded. I confided in her, prayed with her, and loved her. We were good for each other and have been for over forty years.

One of our goals in ministry was to become friends with whoever God brought into our lives. Throughout this tremendous growth period in the Ravenna Church, businessmen in this little town of 11,000 people got to know Lee. This opened up many doors of opportunity to both of us. Lee became a member of the Rotary Club and within two years became president.

"Sharon (here it goes again), it is the custom for the president's wife to be the Rotary Anns' president."

"What does that mean?" I asked with a huge question-mark-looking face.

"That means you will head up all programs for the wives of the Rotarians for one year."

"I can't do that, I've never done anything like that in my life!"

"All you have to do is conduct a meeting with the women once a month, plan a place and program." Once again my husband tried to tell me how qualified I was and I would have no problem at all.

Lord, I don't even know any of these women. Who am I to lead? "Can I think about it?" I asked

"Well, it is pretty much a done deal," Lee answered.

After all of the doubts, it was perhaps one of the most interesting, enjoyable ways of organizing, planning, and meeting with the townswomen. They even asked us to provide the music for the Christmas Banquet. Lee played several instruments: baritone, trombone, electric steel guitar, and had an outstanding baritone voice. I, in turn, played piano, organ, clarinet (not great in any of it), but I did have some voice training, which helped.

Our lives at this time ran full speed ahead. Another event that Lee and I attended was the Ministers' Monthly Fellowship Meeting, held in different churches. The wives were expected to attend unless they worked an outside job. The meetings included a brief message of encouragement. This brought ministers and their wives together for a time of fellowship and singing. However, I sat in fear each time the leader asked, "Is there anyone here who could play the piano for our worship time?"

My head went down to my chest and I would stop breathing. I had great anxiety because I was not a pianist, only played by ear with chords. I had to play an introduction and read music.

"My wife Sharon can play." Lee beamed.

I froze up. *What? "Lord, how can he do this? He thinks I can play, but I can NOT!* Thoughts flooded my emotions as I slowly walked toward the piano. As I sat down on the bench, thoughts raced through my mind. *Why didn't I practice more when my mother made charts to encourage practicing? Why did I beg to switch from piano to clarinet? Why didn't I take more lessons in college?* I could only play well if I knew the song in the key of C, F, or G and only one flat.

My prayer would be: *Help! God, please speak to the song leader to lead page 111, the song "At Calvary." I know that song and play it by ear.*

If the song leader chose a song with four flats, I would just go numb and stumble through. How embarrassing! If I was struggling, I would look up at the song leader as if to say: *Please go ahead and start singing. That was the introduction like it or not.*

This scenario repeated until I got half-way acceptable at playing more songs. As years passed, I did improve but never became an accomplished pianist.

After this public humiliation, there was little left to embarrass me. Back in the 1960s, the pastor's wife was expected to play the piano, sing alto, and be on hand for anything someone else couldn't do. She was expected to be a stay-at-home mom and wear many hats of employment without pay.

My way of dealing with things that stretched me beyond my comfort zone included: sulking, pouting, getting quiet, cleaning, and staying busy. This way, the negatives became less. Working off of adrenaline and replacing the negative with the positive became a full-time job for me.

One example would be when I found out my older sister had a heart attack and didn't pull through, I took our bedroom curtains down, washed them, and hung them back up. Cleaning became one of my replacements. I'm still wondering if this is an escape rather than a replacement.

Facing deep emotions is difficult. My thoughts were if you don't face the emotional stuff, it never happened. Not a very good way to deal with life. This replacement strategy was not a long-term solution.

I never stopped praying and reading the Word. I never forgot that God created me and therefore understood me much better than I did. I would often write encouraging tips for my own encouragement. I saved all of them in hopes of one day helping others with them.

Nature (genetics), nurture (environment), and mindfulness (emotion) make up each of us. God then takes this "glob" and tries to make it into His image. We have to be willing, resourceful, and knowledgeable of God's Word. Overcoming all of this junk is a partnership between God and self. One assurance I have in writing this book is no one is allowed to judge me.

(Dear friends of Sharon,) **Judge not, that ye be not judged. For with what judgment ye judge, ye shall be judged: and with what measure ye mete, it shall be measured to you again. And why beholdest thou the mote that is in thy brother's eye, but considerest not the beam that is in thine own eye? Matthew 7:1-3 [KJV]**

Sorry about that, my friends, if you are reading and judging me. I am not a perfect pastor's wife. None are perfect, however, we strive to become like Him—not judging, only loving.

My dear Father in Heaven, How thankful I am that You are always there for my prayers. I must ask Your forgiveness once again for having a hard time giving up my learned behaviors. I know You understand where I have come from, where I Am and where You want me to be. I feel I am learning to be comfortable in my own skin. Thank You for having patience with me as I strive to turn my weaknesses into strengths. I love You with all of my heart believing that You accept me just as I am. May Your name be glorified, Amen.

Sharon Lebsack

Chapter 8
God's Bonus

Life is a lesson that molds us into who we become. ~Sharon Lebsack

As I learned about DNA, I knew God created me with my own unique personality. However, the environment and how I was raised also influenced who I am. As a result of our circumstances and choices, God creates bonuses to add to our DNA. Born shy, I chose to be an overachiever. Being a pastor's wife has molded me yet further. God has a plan to mold me into the vessel He created me to be. The question was, and is, will I make the right choices? The God bonus in my life was, and is still, unfolding into who God created me to be—the God bonus to our DNA is in Isaiah.

Even every one that is called by my name: for I have created him for my glory, I have formed him; yea, I have made him. Isaiah 43:7 [KJV]

I was raised almost as an only child. My adult sister and brother were married and starting their own families when I was born. The first time I heard my dad mention my being shy, it changed me. I overheard him say to my mother, "I'm concerned about Sharon being so shy. How will she make it in life?"

I know he didn't expect me to hear, nor did he mean harm, he was just concerned. However, those words changed who I am. They have flooded my being throughout my lifetime. I felt compelled to prove I would make it in life. Consequently, I have always set high goals of reaching my mark, of being acceptable, focused on giving my highest effort. This could have been a weakness, but God used it as a strength. Although going overboard in all things makes for a crowded life, multitasking became a way of life as I tried to be my best in whatever came my way.

My mother called me one late afternoon and, in the course of our conversation, she asked me what I was doing. I replied, "Mopping the floor, getting dinner, and making a pie."

"What?" Surprise sounded in her voice. "All at the same time?"

"I have to, Mom. This is my life."

On another occasion, one of our pastor friends stopped by unexpectedly. We had a short visit, however, when he left, I realized my floor had not been mopped that day. I was humiliated. My goal was to have my house clean and orderly, when, and if anyone came to my door. I had myself convinced that the pastor's home and family, should be guest-ready at all times. That also went for my appearance, guest-ready any time of the day. After all, this is expected—isn't it?

The CHALLENGE you are presently facing is where God wants you to learn and become like Him. It's your chance to prove God. There are three phases we face in life:

- Mountaintop Highs

- Foot of the Mountain Lows
- Climbing the Mountain Everyday

Climbing the Mountain is a healthy place to be—this is "real life." We have been on a Mountaintop place for several years. Often sliding back to the Foot of the Mountain, we long to climb.

I've often thought of the children's story "The Little Engine That Could." The engine said, "I think I can. I think I can." If you are huffing and puffing, "I think I can" and want to climb that mountain, then take these steps:

Stand up and walk. – Ask God for help.

Eat – Take nourishment from the Word.

Change – Thought patterns from "I can't!" to "I can!"

Trust God – To be your mountain-climbing companion.

In that small town of 11,000 people, God did a mighty work. In fact, it was a miracle. Lee became President of the Ministerial Organization. Having association with pastors and priests was good for him. If we took time off to look at this picture of life, I'm sure we would have been overwhelmed, but we just kept taking steps toward the doors God was opening. "For such a time as this," became a reality in our lives, as we became aware this was the time God had orchestrated this phenomenal church growth.

Lee, our staff, and leadership organized contests, programs, teaching, and training to motivate our congregation to win this city for our Lord. The scripture, **Go into all the world and preach the gospel to all creation. Mark 16:15 [NIV]** became a reality in our church family. Where there's a call, there is a vision, and without a vision, the people perish.

The years passed quickly with new converts, new families, and new staff members. Once again, as in Vermilion, we had outgrown our program. We started having Sunday school classes in offices, overcrowded rooms, and eventually had to use our home. At this point, Lee went to the church board and asked if they would consider making the parsonage an extension of our church. He went on to suggest giving us a financial raise to buy our own home. They were in total agreement. Tonya's favorite song was, "There's a change made since I've been born, there's a change made since I've been born. There's a change made since I've been born. There's a change made since I've been born again." Change is a good thing if you make it a good thing, so that's what we did.

We were thrilled to find a move-in-ready home which was good because we had no time to fix up a home. With the school only a few blocks from our new home, the girls made friends in the neighborhood. Our own home made me feel more secure.

Before I got too comfortable, Lee again came to me with a request. "Sharon, let's talk!"

I knew what this meant by now. With this visionary man I married, I had to be prepared at all times.

"TV," he said. I waited for more, and he just looked at me with a mischievous sparkle in his eyes. "The elders and board have decided this would be a great extension of our church for getting the word out about Jesus and His plan for humanity."

"And the name of the program is," Lee said with a smile, "'Christ is the Answer.'" It will be a weekly telecast with both of us hosting a talk show on current subjects, along with three musical renditions between breaks, orchestrated by our minister of music, Eddy Hawks."

I've learned not to be surprised about anything this man would come up with in his quest to reach this generation for Christ. If the church could not cover the cost of this home mission's project, we would not do it. There would be no gimmicks or asking for money from the TV audience. I was in agreement with the new adventure.

God made it all happen, and I loved being a part of this program. Lee consented for me to get the material for the program so I would be comfortable with the topics. We taught topics such as loss, fear, contentment, joy, unanswered prayer, healing, baptism, and many more relevant subjects. The response was overwhelming. People from other towns who watched our TV program came to visit and many joined our congregation.

With the TV program, our seventy-five-year-old church in this little town grew rapidly. God made history in our church as He turned my weaknesses into strengths. He did this not because of who I am, but because of who He is. None of this would have happened if Lee hadn't needed help in growing our churches. Never in a million years had I thought I could ever be more than a mother and housewife. That alone is a high calling, but to share Jesus on TV and see the results in new members brought me a new thrill.

Soon some of my "fill-in" duties were being filled by others. I had more time and confidence. The puzzles of my life seemed to be fitting together. I grew accustomed to "busyness" and looked forward to every waking moment. To this day, I'm so very thankful for rest and sleep, but dread going to bed at night because life stops. This was all God's plan.

Approximately every six months to a year, the "busyness" would catch up with me and I would crash. When the red flags, such as sadness, withdrawal, defensiveness, and anxiety, waved before me I knew I had to regroup. I never wanted to stop because of the high I would get from adrenaline rushes.

Our lives at times reminded me of a gerbil or hamster spinning on that wire wheel in the cage. This was exactly like my life; the only difference was my personality did not know when to stop to take a break. It seemed about once a year red flags waved a warning to stop and rest. I know what is required of me as a wife, mother, friend and pastor's wife—it's important. Of course, the red flags shouted, *You're tired, feeling self-pity, and used. You're getting grouchy, especially with your family. You need a break. Am I really bringing glory to God on this wheel?* I couldn't seem to get off of the spinning wheel. I even knew these warning flags would eventually bring burn-out, weariness, self-pity, blaming others—all blooming forth into oppression.

Over time, I discovered that after I pushed through the exhaustion point, I would get a surge of energy. Of course, this was an unhealthy energy, my heart would beat faster and the inside of me felt like a wild woman. This was not good and not safe. I recalled a time when some of the women on our staff and I would be playing tennis. Even though they were younger than me, I prided myself in having the energy to keep playing when they would be tired and lying out on the court. Was this good? I still don't know the answer to how far we can/should push ourselves. I had to find a way out of this cage.

Loving me, pouring His grace down on me, God planted a

desire. I needed to visit my parents by myself. I needed a break, a rest, and deliberation with God.

Lee and I had a heart-to-heart concerning my going to my parents'. Would he be OK with the girls staying here? Any husband who is close and caring of his wife would recognize signs of exhaustion. Lee is definitely one.

He came toward me, giving me a hug. "Sharon, I know you need a break from everything and we will get along just fine. We'll all miss you, but we can do this for a week. You go and receive the downtime which you need. You deserve it."

Immediately, a feeling of release came over me and I broke down with tears of brokenness representing relief, sadness, happiness, guilt, and much more. I usually only cry when I feel defeated, perplexed, helpless, or derailed.

After taking care of arrangements around the house and creating a schedule for the girls, I packed my bag. The next morning I loaded my car and made the six-hour drive to my parents' home. I relaxed to easy-listening radio and enjoyed the scenery. When I arrived, I took a deep breath, feeling a surge of energy over my entire body, soul, and spirit.

As I entered through the door, the aroma of homemade apple pie went straight to my brain. Mom and dad greeted me with hugs of happiness. Mom made my favorite meal at that time—fried chicken, mashed potatoes with gravy, green beans, and of course there was indeed homemade apple pie.

The time I spent with my parents and God during this time changed my inner feelings from tsunami to ripples of peace. I didn't need a spa or a cruise. I just needed a quiet, peaceful, comfortable place to read God's Word, meditate, and regroup.

How does this miracle happen? Here I am an adult and my parents are aged, but still loving, caring, and giving. Yet, when it came time for me to leave, I was ready. I received what I came for at the peaceful home of my parents. Ready to return home to my family, I wasn't the same as when I left. God's word and meditation showed me how to regroup, replace, and restore. The hugs of my parents offered me a place to rest.

On the drive back home, I saw a plan—ways to get off that spinning wheel. As I drove up to our home, I saw Lee and the girls out by our pool. A smile came with the thought *I am such a blessed woman!*

The family wanted to hear about my week with their grandma and grandpa. Then I wanted to hear about their week with Mr. Mom. I found out they ate out every night and had ice cream after church on Wednesday night. Tami blurted out, "Dad didn't take us to piano lessons." I looked at him with raised eyebrows, but they deserved a break, too. The girls smiled from ear-to-ear as they turned and jumped into the pool.

I was overtaken with surprise when Lee went into the house and brought a piece of paper out to read to me. On this paper were things that he had thought of that might give me a head start in regrouping my life.

1. Take a day for me once a week.
2. Have a downtime each day to meditate.
3. Find outside projects to bring fulfillment, such as refinishing old pieces of furniture, scrapbooking, and more alone projects.

In other words, take time for diversions with things that

bring fulfillment to me as an individual. It was amazing when we compared our lists. Mine consisted of:

1. Visit the elderly
2. Find a volunteer group that reaches out to unwed mothers.
3. Start a program for sending cards or calling on the sick.

You get the idea. Yes, these were things I could do that would be different from the usual. These things were ministry-related. Lee's list was also ministry-related, but different. They ministered to me. I thought it selfish to do anything just for me. But the Father in heaven took time away from ministering throughout His 33 years on earth. Two verses in the Bible stood out to me as I sought for answers of WWJD (What would Jesus do?)

But Jesus often withdrew to lonely places and prayed. Luke 5:16 [NIV]

Once again Jesus went out beside the lake. Mark 2:13 [NIV]

This was a learning time for me and even though I no doubt will continue to struggle with MY weaknesses, I now have this time to reflect back on. It is giving me a new meaning for life. My life has always been husband and family first, which included a peaceful and orderly home with time for family interaction, three meals a day prepared and served.

Right now you are saying: "Sharon, all women do this, not just pastors' wives." True, but it became an obsession to me. There was no room for omission of anything. In the meantime there are phone calls, counseling sessions, attendance in every church service and event, committees, filling in when needed. I can't name them all. This is expected of every pastor's wife. I'm not whining, I'm just relating the guilt I felt if I didn't do it all. After all, I did put this upon myself, didn't I? Now was the time to get a grip on my weakness. It was all done for God—maybe yes, maybe no. Was I out to prove I could do it all? Probably. Was I driven by trying to prove and please? Probably. Is this healthy? Probably not! I wanted to support and be a helpmate to Lee.

I wanted everyone to love us. After all, we loved everyone and were working diligently to build this church with unity and growth. Three words summed up my life at this particular time: rejection, resentment, and restoration.

Rejection left unchecked would grow into pulling away, feeling insecure, and leave me unable to be authentic with others. Resentment created an attitude that people would sense. I had to constantly battle these emotions. Restoration came when I gave the emotions to the Lord and waited for His game plan.

It took me quite a while to get to the point where I could say, "I'm doing this for God, not man." It became much easier and I felt less resentful, more willing to do whatever God asked of me.

Following God's plan meant being on the alert for someone who needed encouragement. I felt attracted to those who were sad, lonely or discouraged. This was a calling. No doubt God sent these dear ones into my life to prove to me that God would use me to make a difference in the life of others. It became quite clear when I reached out to encourage someone, that I, too, was encouraged.

"Give, and it shall be given unto you..." Luke 6:38 [KJV]

This verse became a reality in my thought process. My love and teaching for women came directly from God's Word. I soon realized many women never had a mentor for learning how to be a godly wife and mother. They often had no family support, nor could they provide family support to their own family. This became a cause for me. I began to feel my gifts had developed and with them, joy and fulfillment settled in my heart.

In the process of this great growth spurt, we had to consider building a new facility. Through several financial blessings from our congregation and community, a six-acre plot of land on a major highway was given to us, along with enough money to build a new facility seating over 1,000 in the auditorium.

However, with growth comes challenge. It seems there is always a group of disgruntled people who feel the need to complain about something. Of course, in a growing church, when God is miraculously building His church, these people may be disruptive in an ungodly manner.

"Does the pastor really need another home?"

"Do we really need a new building?"

Most of the time, these complaints are about the pastor, his vision, and his decisions. These complaints, even though just a few, upset me. Instead of going to the pastor, much of the time people would share with me some of the comments. After all, I'm the pastor's wife.

One of my favorite exercises is to go to God's Word and find a passage where it would address exactly what I was going through. Some of those passages are found in Exodus.

God will lead His people. (13:18)

God will take care of you. (13:19)

The Lord will go before you. (13:21)

God knows the enemy. (14:3)

God is always in control. (14:4)

God always has a plan and it will work. (14:8)

You may feel defeated, but you are not. (14:9)

If fear does set in, always cry out to God. (14:10)

Questioning God usually follows fear. (14:11)

The Lord will fight for you; you need only to be still. (14:14)

In spite of the complaints, the Ravenna miracle continued at the new location with the influx of people coming to the altar for salvation. The great spirit in the church poured down with salvation, life-changing faith and much more.

God, am I the right person for this plan that's unfolding? Are you sure I can handle everything on my plate?

His answer was always in a subtle, quiet manner.

A couple of months before my birthday, I looked in the mirror and a thought popped into my head. A strong desire for a pair of small diamond earrings pushed my-I-want-button. I had one diamond and it was my wedding ring. I had never asked for diamonds nor had any desire for any, until that day.

I didn't ask God for them, I only had the fleeting desire. As I stood there looking at my ears, I felt strongly that I wouldn't ask Lee for this gift. If I didn't ask him, of course, I wouldn't get them. Lee's mind didn't dwell on his wife's earrings. So there, that's it! The desire was as strong as I ever felt for anything. Strange, yes, because I rarely asked for anything expensive. I forgot about that desire until one night while attending a missions' benefit at the Broadmoor Hotel in Colorado Springs, Colorado.

Author and Pastor, Tommy Barnett, founder of Dream City Church, spoke that night on missions. A couple Lee and I knew were seated at our table with four other people. After the close of the service, while still sitting at the table, my friend thoughtfully looked at me. Causally, she took off her earrings and reaching toward me, placed them in my hand.

"God told me to give these to you."

Stunned, I couldn't speak. Did she read my mind? Was this a magic trick? The way she phrased her words made me know it was God—nothing but God. He told her to give me the earrings. A desire of my heart—God telling me He knew where I was in life. He gave me a desire of my heart to let me know He was pleased with my faithfulness, trust, and love.

Father in heaven, I am amazed at how You know me, not only by name, but You know my every thought. I want to give You praise and thanksgiving for letting me see that You know me, even more than my earthly father. I love You and am so privileged to have You as my heavenly Father. In Your Son's name, Amen.

Sharon Lebsack

Chapter 9

A Bend in the Dream

Prayer should never be a last resort…pray first. ~Sharon Lebsack

A Disturbing Incident - Shortly before we left Ravenna, there was a very disturbing incident that we would remember for years to come. Lee was in his office one morning and a lady who was very active in the church wanted spiritual counsel. This woman was married, had children and had come to confess of an affair with a man in the community. She sobbed while telling how this affair came about and she wanted to end it, but the man did not. Lee's advice, from God's Word, was to stop the affair immediately, confess to God and to her husband.

This woman proceeded to call the man to end their adulterous affair. He became livid when she told him of her council with her pastor (Lee). He came to the church office the next day to let his anger out on Lee. He pinned him up against the wall telling him he knew that Lee knew about this affair and if He EVER told any person any of this he would shoot him.

Lee looked pale, his expression worried when he came home that night. He told me about the incident in a soft, restrained voice.

"What are you going to do?" I asked.

"Pray!" My husband had just been threatened by a man who promised to shoot him if he leaked their story. This incident left a memory that we will never forget. It could have easily been carried out. However, God is in control and has not given us a spirit of fear.

I've always heard that the life of a minister is one of the most difficult professions for the man and wife. The church is our extended family and they depend on us as their pastors, counselors, and teachers. Many think they are the only ones with issues. Others feel we are "super people." There are those who don't want to bother us because they think their problems may be too small compared to the tremendous responsibility we bear. However, we are just ordinary people called by God to help and encourage as we can. There are no perfect people in or outside of the ministry.

Once you follow God's calling, you will never want to do it any other way. God showed me a chapter in Joshua and it certainly hit home of how to follow His plan in this next move. Anyone making a decision in their life can use this formula set by God for Joshua.

In the book of Joshua, the third chapter, we see the new leader, Joshua, getting ready to lead the Israelites across the Jordan River. God divided the waters at the Jordan just as He did at the Red Sea for Moses. Joshua followed His directions. God went before him, leading, directing, and guiding all the way.

1. Joshua 3:3 – **FOLLOW THE ARK** – Keep in God's presence at all times.

2. Joshua 3:5 – **CONSECRATE YOURSELVES** – Search your heart for any sinful nature and ask God's forgiveness.

3. Joshua 3:6 – **MAKE A DECISION** – To move, make changes, and travel a new direction in your life with God as your guide.

4. Joshua 3:7 – **GOD PROMISES TO BE WITH YOU.**

5. Joshua 3:8 - **STAND STILL NOW AND WATCH, LOOK, AND LISTEN.**

6. Joshua 3:9 – **HEAR THE WORD OF GOD.**

7. Joshua 3:10 - **THE BATTLE IS THE LORD'S** - We do our part and He does His part. We can't do His part and He can't do our part.

8. Joshua 3:11 – **THE LORD WILL GO AHEAD OF YOU** – Don't miss recognizing Him and following Him.

9. Joshua 3:13-16 - **VICTORY! STEP IN AND CROSS OVER"** - We always have to take the first step.

Both Lee and I had been in agreement each time we moved in ministry and this was no different. We felt in our hearts this was the right move but didn't think the girls would be as excited. Tami was thirteen and Tonya ten. Happy in school and church, they both had a lot of friends and we assumed it might be hard for them to make this big move.

We took this situation to God in prayer asking Him to prepare the girls to hear of our latest news.

Before we made the trip to South Bend, we wanted to tell them. I remember this talk distinctly. It happened one Saturday morning as we sat at the breakfast table. Lee explained our new move. As he talked, Tami interrupted.

"Dad, I had a dream last week that we moved to a different town, a new church, and school. Tami's eyes brighten with God-inspired excitement as she continued, "In my dream, I made new friends and was so happy. I didn't realize this was really going to happen."

God is so good! By now Tonya was getting excited and we all felt the move was right in our spirits. These confirmations made us feel even better about our decision.

After ten years in Ravenna, I recognized God's quiet voice in preparing us for another move in ministry. Pastor Jack West in South Bend, Indiana called Lee to ask if he would consider the position of lead pastor of the South Bend church. We should not have been shocked at a request because we had been praying and seeking God's plan. Pastor West was retiring. He invited us to come for an interview with the elders and board members. It was the history of this church that the pastor who was leaving would select the next pastor. We found a weekend on our calendar that would work and scheduled the interview.

With a couple of weeks to talk about this next possible move in our ministry, we prayed. Change faced our family very soon.

Dear Father in Heaven, My heart is full as I look back over the ten years in Ravenna, Ohio. I would never have believed such miracles could take place under our ministry. You never cease to amaze me with how Your Word reflects who You are and who I am. Thank You for being patient with me, instructing me, and giving me a husband who understands me. I am not the perfect pastor's wife, but I'm learning how to practice Your word. I pray that Lee and I will always be at a place where we can hear Your voice. Amen.

Sharon Lebsack

Part Three

South Bend, Indiana

A Bend in the road is not the end of the road-unless you fail to make the turn. ~Helen Keller

Sharon Lebsack

Chapter 10

Around the Bend

What you fill your day with is who you are. ~ Sharon Lebsack

As the day approached when Lee and I made the drive to South Bend, we continued to feel God's plan unfolding. We knew how different this city would be from Ravenna where there were only four stop lights, three restaurants, one dress shop and two grocery stores. A town of over 100,000 residents excited Lee. Not only 100,000 souls to hear of God's love, but South Bend was the home of Notre Dame University, well-known for their sports program. Lee was a fan, and South Bend was a home run for him.

We arrived at the church for the meeting with Pastor West and the three-lifetime elders and seventeen board members. While in the conference room, deep into the interview, the phone rang in the office. Pastor West answered it and a huge smile appeared on his face.

"Yes, yes, that sounds wonderful and you will not believe it but we are interviewing him and his wife as we speak." When he got off the phone, he explained the conversation. "That was Dr. E.M. Clark, president of North Central Bible College recommending we consider Lee Lebsack to become lead pastor." What a surprise to all of us as this seemed to be the final confirmation, perhaps the handwriting on the wall. We left that meeting ready for a full weekend of interviews, dinners, searching for a house, and looking over the town.

On Sunday morning, Lee brought forth the message to the congregation. The church membership voted on the new pastor and Lee received 100 percent agreement. It just felt right!

My head was spinning as I considered everything that had to be done before we moved. The following week, Lee gave the church board in Ravenna his letter of resignation and announced his resignation to the congregation that Sunday. It would be sad to leave this church, but when God has a plan for us to move on, we follow.

There was a farewell service with singing, sharing memories, and time for final goodbyes. Many members of the community came to our farewell. It was bittersweet, but all the time we were confident in knowing this was God's time for change. We had found a house in South Bend that the girls were going to love because it had a swimming pool and a basketball court. The girls would each have their own room and they could decorate them like they wanted. The youth group had written to Tami saying they were excited for her to be part of their youth program. She couldn't wait to get there to meet her new friends.

Church lore defines the first two years for a new pastor as a honeymoon and that was true in South Bend. The board agreed for us to bring our staff from Ravenna. That was a blessing since we had formed bonds with each staff member. Lee had mentored these men and I met with their wives once a month to share challenges and pray together. It's amazing how God can encourage us when we form a support group of godly women who share and pray together through different challenges of ministry. We understand each other.

Finally, I had a glimpse of the big picture and I saw what God had prepared for me.

Maybe I was ready for the birthing of my purpose. Thinking back over the past thirteen years, I understood it all had been preparation—being molded by the Master.

When a woman gives birth, she has a hard time, there's no getting around it. But when the baby is born, there is joy in the birth. This new life in the world wipes out memory of the pain. The sadness you may have right now is similar to that pain, but the coming joy is also similar.

When I see you again, you'll be full of joy and it will be a joy no one can rob from you. You'll no longer be full of questions. John 16:21-23 [MSG]

Through life's challenges as a pastor's wife, God had been birthing my purpose in life. The teaching and training from God now pushed me to the point of delivering this gift (my purpose). I no longer felt the pain of labor in this development of my gift. I knew the job was not complete, there was still more valley experiences that would lead me further in developing my spiritual muscles.

Sharon Lebsack

(Sharon,) **That's plain enough, isn't it? You're no longer wandering exiles. This kingdom of faith is now your home country. You're no longer strangers or outsiders. You belong here, with as much right to the name Christian as anyone. God is building a home. He's using us all—irrespective of how we got here—in what he is building. He used the apostles and prophets for the foundation. Now he's using you, fitting you in brick by brick, stone by stone, with Christ Jesus as the cornerstone that holds all the parts together. We see it taking shape day after day—a holy temple built by God, all of us built into it, a temple in which God is quite at home. Ephesians 2:19-21 [MSG]**

The church in South Bend was well-established, with faithful leadership. Consequently, I did not have to fill in for various positions. I know now that the objective was for me to be refined and poured into God's mold, not mine. In the process of refining gold, we see some pretty graphic steps. Think of how they relate to God's molding His followers.

One day, as I was meditating on the different issues and challenges in my life, I started to see a timeline in my life. I'm not saying this is for everyone, but it was a bright light for me. There are several reasons for trials and tribulations coming into our lives. Surely if God loved us it would be all smooth sailing, right? Well, no, it doesn't work like that. I've discovered He uses circumstances to grow us, perhaps to get our attention to trust Him, and sometimes life just happens. This has helped me understand the scripture in Romans 8:28 that God works all things together for good. In order for His plan and purpose for our lives to unfold, we may have to go through a few trials and tribulations. In order to get through these trying times, I've used the following plan to help me "get a grip."

PRAYER

1. Petition to God for Him to walk with me on this path.

2. Request my husband join me in prayer.

3. Ask a close, trusting friend to join me in prayer.

JOURNAL

1. Make notes during my devotional time.

2. Journal my feelings. (Which could be used in a book years down the line.)

READ SCRIPTURE

1. Sometimes just open up the Bible and start reading.

2. Look up different subjects (Examples: change, joy, contentment, love, serving, loss, death, rejection, and more.) in the Bible to find God's resolution.

MEDITATION

1. Practice meditation: "meditate day and night."

2. Meditation relieves anxiety and stress.

3. I found the words in my prayer were basically to build my faith along with petitioning Jesus, sitting at the right hand of the Father, to make intercession for me. Then meditation became God speaking to me. **Prayer was from me to God—meditation was from God to me.**

4. It took me years to learn the concept of meditation. I find walking, surrounded by God's nature clears my mind and I truly hear from God. At the fitness center while working out on the elliptical machine, I've found that ideas, and answers to relevant issues in my life, stream into my mind.

5. Train your mind to listen and replace your negative thoughts and feelings with the positive. Our mind can only think one thought at a time, so changing the negative into a positive eliminates the negative.

REACHING OUT TO OTHERS

1. Encouraging women whenever opportunities come up.
2. Organize a support group for "Women Encouraging Women."
3. Be available to mentor young women.

Sharon's ways to reach out to others:

- Wrote a monthly email blog "Encouraging Notes" and sent around the world.
- Wrote and produced a parent/teen video series.
- Authored a mentoring booklet.
- Authored a girl's retreat booklet.
- Authored a lifestyle eating and exercise plan.

After reflecting on the Timelines of my life, I realized out of dry-gulch-experiences, God brought about illuminating results for me to share with others. Through prayer, meditation, and action, doors would open up daily for me to get my mind off of myself and onto others. Consequently, I am no doubt blessed beyond my ability to bless others. Try it, you'll like it.

Our Father which art in Heaven, may praise be to Your name. As I search my heart, I find I have so much more to learn about becoming the person You created me to be. I understand I have to go through trials and temptations while on this earth. I'm asking You to forgive my stubborn ways, my controlling spirit, and thoughts of defeat. Help me to see Your ways, not my ways and to think Your thoughts, not my thoughts. Forgive me for my faults, while I forgive those offending me, for You would not lead us into temptation, but deliver us from evil. Lead me in paths of righteousness for Your name's sake. May I never disappoint You as a wife to Lee, mother to our children, a mentor to others, and a pastor's wife to our congregation. I will try my best to not disappoint the One who created me for His purpose and plan for my life.

In Jesus' name, Amen.

Sharon Lebsack

Chapter 11
A Bend in the Road

"Jesus promised his disciples three things—that they would be completely fearless, absurdly happy, and in constant trouble."
~ Barclay

Life was moving fast with settling in, enrolling the girls in school, and getting the house in order. It seemed our family was a perfect fit for the church in South Bend. The congregation was so welcoming and willing to follow Lee's vision. Excitement filled the air and things seemed great, but when a hiccup hits you lose momentum and your focus is interrupted from the routine of ministry. Sometimes these situations have been allowed by God to get our attention. I've often reminded Lee to keep our eyes and ears open to God, so He doesn't have to get our attention.

One evening, the phone rang. It was usually for me, but I would always try to get Lee or the girls to answer. I picked up the phone only to hear our youth pastor telling me of a very upsetting situation.

"Sharon, I hate that I have to call you and Pastor about Tami, but I feel it is very important. When you dropped her off for our youth event last night, she got in an older boy's car and sped off, returning about an hour later."

My heart jumped up in my throat. I called Lee to the phone and had him finish the conversation. Tami was fourteen at the time and knew she was not allowed to date until she turned sixteen. She was quite aware that she was never to get in a car with anyone without our consent, especially teen drivers.

Lee and I first discussed the issue and made a decision on what to do about it. We waited until the next night to approach the subject. We had prayed, talked through the situation, and came up with a plan. Whenever we had an issue to deal with in our family or church challenges, we would discuss, pray, compromise, and come to an agreement. We could then ask the Father, Son, and Holy Spirit to join us in addressing any situation.

My interpretation of Matthew 5:24 is intended to make things right with each other and be in agreement before coming to God for direction. God wants me to leave my gift to Him in front of the altar and be reconciled to my husband and then come and offer my gift to him.

The plan was for Lee to take Tami to our downstairs family room. He would talk to her about the incident and I would be upstairs praying. Tonya was always quiet, studying the situation, learning from watching and listening. She was a very smart little girl. She loved her sister and knew of this issue. After about half an hour I heard them coming up the stairs with Tami going straight to her room. I looked at Lee and he gave me a "thumbs up." The consequences presented were to have no contact with this boy ever again. She was too young, the boy was too old for her, and a rule had been broken. Tami was heartbroken but chose to accept the consequences. Lee told me she was remorseful and after the discussion, they hugged and prayed together.

At times like this, I felt like everyone in the church knew about this incident when, in reality, only a few knew. Nonetheless, it made my heart sad because we were supposed to have a "perfect family." Knowing that the perfect family thing was impossible, I had to get over this feeling. Perfect was not then, nor is it now, humanly possible. I couldn't put this pressure on our girls at times like this because it was a teaching and training time for our family. We had to work daily to have a marriage and family that would be pleasing to God. My part was to leave man out of the picture. Lee was always confident at times like this, after all, we were not perfect and neither was our family. We just wanted to do our part with God as our judge, mentor, counselor, and instructor at these times.

SURPRISE!

During our second year in South Bend, the vision for our city came into a focused reality. Lee preached amazing sermons and taught from the Word. We had a wonderful worship team, a TV show, and great leaders with the same vision of reaching our community for Christ. I felt my gifts were being used. I had a heart for women in general and especially women in ministry. I had been chosen to serve on the board for Women's Ministry with a qualified, godly woman as president. The board and I would meet quarterly to plan for the year. The president was in charge of monthly meetings, women's retreats, Bible studies, and classes for women's issues. I soon saw a need for M.O.P.S. (mothers of preschoolers). This program served as a great tool for our community, and women started attending. I loved working with women as the overseer of all of their events. My purpose formed right before my eyes. It felt right.

As different districts started hearing of my encouragement to women in ministry, I received invitations to speak at retreats, seminars, women's groups, and many state programs for pastors' wives. This was my heart. It proved to also be an outlet for me in my role as a pastor's wife. I would hear of the challenges these women had of balancing home, jobs, staff, family, trying to please everyone, and still have time to have a healthy relationship with their husbands. Many wanted out of the ministry, others were even contemplating leaving their husband because of defeat. I shared how I got through it all and tried to lace the stories with humor—hurt, mean people, depression, self-pity, plus physical and emotional ailments.

I woke up one day feeling frantic. There were symptoms which led me to believe I might be pregnant. I thought, oh my, how could this be happening? I shared this imminent possibility with Lee and he seemed to be excited. Really? I could not imagine going through a pregnancy at forty-one years of age. I had two teenagers and the thought of starting over with a new infant overwhelmed me. I began picturing our home with a crib, high chair, potty chair, and all the new "equipment" we would need for a baby. I would be on duty 24/7 for the diaper changes and feedings. How would I still have time for my husband and two teenage daughters? How could I continue with my new-found women's ministry?

Tears mingled with sobs of "I can't do this!" *But God, how can I handle this challenge?* I recalled that my mother was forty when she had me. Still, thoughts of how would I cope with this kept running through my mind. After getting the confirmation from the doctor, I realized that this was just another one of God's plans. I set out to reaffirm that I could do this. I had learned from past situations.

One day, as I contemplated our life, I called the church office and asked to speak to Lee. I never bothered or bugged him so he always took my call, no matter what was happening in his office. My voice was shaking as I blurted out, "Come and get me! I have to talk, but not at home." Within fifteen minutes he was home, bursting through the door, asking what was wrong. He could tell by the look on my face and the tears streaming down that it was serious. We got in the car and he drove off.

As I gained my composure, I started telling him all of the things over the past twenty years that had bothered me in our marriage, all the things I kept bottled up inside. Because I had never acted or talked about this openly before, he was in shock. I told him I could not keep these things inside anymore. As I blurted out my hurts we were both crying. He let me totally unload, my pain spewing out like an erupting volcano.

It felt good but again, it felt awful. I didn't want to hurt Lee. I told him how much I loved him. Then I said, "Now you tell me things in our marriage that you've kept inside that you didn't like." As I looked at him, I could see the hurt in his eyes.

"There is nothing," he muttered. I turned toward him in my seat.

"That is not true! I know there are things you did not like that I did. You have let me unload all of my stuff, now it's your turn." I stared at him. "I'm listening."

With the kindest, most gentle, loving voice, he looked at me exclaiming, "I love you, so those things don't count. I look over them because I love you!"

"That's not fair!" I shouted and cried more.

The title of this book is *Confessions of a Pastor's Wife*. After reading the above paragraph, you, the reader, might be thinking, "*Okay, confess, Sharon! What are some of the things that you kept hidden for twenty years?*"

One of those hidden secrets was how my childhood left an imprint of not raising voices. I never heard my mother and father raise their voices to each other or to me. Lee's family spoke on several levels louder than mine. Consequently, when Lee would speak to me at different times in a raised voice, I would feel attacked. Touchy? Maybe, but it just hurt as I felt I was being talked down to. He assured me this was the way he always spoke.

I did ask one day, "Do you speak to your secretary in that tone?" We both laughed, but Lee got the picture. It was a learned behavior of voice control and would no doubt take time to improve. It did get better as I put the brakes on being the offended, and Lee worked on his part as the offender. It most often is the little things that bring huge outcry. However "it's the little things that God uses to change a heart.

We started back home realizing this had been a defining moment for both of us. We knew each other much better now. I was relieved. It set a precedent for more open communication and we truly loved each other. I felt now I could continue on this path of becoming a middle-aged mother married to a middle-aged man. I had the assurance that I could handle the plan God had laid out for me if I would:

- Pray
- Read the Word for encouragement.
- Keep using the gifts God gave me.
- Place positive people in my path.
- Have a plan for the new life. (Change can be good, but it takes planned steps to reach it.)
- Keep communications open with family and friends.

Our third daughter, Tiffany Kate, was born August 14, 1979, and our whole family was thrilled with this new addition. A good baby, Tiffany only woke up every three hours at night. BT (before Tiffany) my daytime job was so different. Instead of getting up at seven in the morning, now I got up at midnight, three, and six in the morning, ready to start my day taking care of our new baby. Did I mention that I am not a morning person? The one big advantage was I decided to nurse this little one, which saved me from formula preparation, getting up to heat bottles, along with washing and sterilizing bottles. A wave of exhilaration swept through me when I realized there were DISPOSABLE diapers, which had not been available for Tami and Tonya.

It seemed I was the only one in our family whose life changed. Lee, Tami, and Tonya got a good night's sleep, got up at the regular time in the morning, and were off to work and school. This pattern seemed okay at first, but then I started feeling trapped.

When they got home from work and school, their lives still went on the same path as BT. I could never leave the house unless I took Tiffany with me or got a babysitter. I really started having a pity party over this situation. I went to God and asked Him specifically how to handle it. Evidently, feeling trapped was my personal issue and one only I had to solve. God, in His wisdom, was working in me and I was putting the brakes on. I had to make changes but didn't have a clue as to how. Eventually, the puzzle came together and I realized Tiffany was born for me. I've often told her this and she no doubt doesn't even understand it—maybe after reading this book, she will. This was a time in my life when I needed a "jump-start" in a new direction. I had never been consistent in journaling (I had plenty of time now). I have heard people talk about meditation, but I never had time to meditate (now I do). The truth be known, I had never sat still long enough to hear the Spirit of God speaking His thoughts, His plan, His direction. Now my life was taking on new meaning in the spiritual realm.

When you are in the kind of servanthood we had chosen,

most of our conversation time is about our family and the church. Lee and I spent 90% of our time communicating about church challenges, issues, new programs, and future plans. Subsequently, there usually was no time for our personal communication. If I felt I needed some quality communication about what was happening in my life, I would say to Lee, "Can we talk?"

He would sigh, "What about?" I knew then it was not the time. After dealing all day with people, he needed a break. What men don't know is that women need communication. Left unattended, this could cause a casualty.

As I continued asking the Holy Spirit to speak to my heart for a solution, I started hearing that still small voice. I felt instructed to call a family meeting, present my petition and let my family know I had these feelings. Did they even realize I was struggling? As we all gathered in the family room, I began sharing my heart.

"I have a problem, and I need your thoughts on how to handle it." As I said those words, tears came. It got very quiet as I explained how I had been feeling and needed some suggestions from them on how to handle this situation because it was going to impact our family life.

Lee spoke first, telling me I needed some outside activities such as tennis or golf. He suggested taking lessons and then we would work on a daytime sitter. Tami and Tonya said they could babysit Tiffany at least once a week. Each of them was brainstorming with me for ideas. My heart raced as I felt their love, concern, and thoughtful suggestions. How I love my family.

I felt really good about the family meeting. Perhaps I had found a way of communicating on personal issues that worked for us. I started putting our brainstorming into a plan and realized it wasn't as big of a conundrum as I thought. In fact, since then I have recommended this way of communication for those who have a hard time resolving controversy. I've given this action point a name—Family Staff Meeting. This works so much better than talking on the run, in the midst of confusion, or when either party is tired or focused on something else that is monopolizing their mind.

I had a start in the right direction, but it took me awhile to orchestrate the plan. Soon I found a tennis teacher and babysitter. I took some lessons and, surprisingly, loved tennis because it was not only a stress release but a diversion and enjoyable. It gave me an opportunity to meet new women, which was another type of reflection. Now my mind was getting into balance and I could think more categorically.

As the weeks progressed I saw how God was using balance to get my attention so He could direct me on this change in my life. He said, *"Sharon, just be still and listen, trust me, I'm taking you into new beginnings."*

Open My Eyes that I Might See

In the book of Luke, we read of the blind man asking Jesus to open his eyes that he might see. Jesus touched his eyes and told him to look, what did he see? We know there was an angry crowd around him. We don't know, do we? Did he see beauty or beast? Did he ignore all of the people, the anger, and see Jesus?

I can ask myself the same question. When I present a petition to Jesus, am I missing the answer? I'm afraid many times I've looked for answers to come in a "box" like I ordered. When Jesus sends His box, He knows what is best for me. The Word of God tells us,

"In all things give thanks; for this is the will of God in Christ Jesus concerning you." I Thessalonians 5:18 [KJV]

Perhaps you have received the answer to your prayer and...

1. You didn't accept it.
2. You didn't recognize it.
3. You're looking for something else.
4. You are so disappointed.
5. You continue praying and begging for something that is already there.
6. You cannot find contentment, joy, and thanksgiving because it's not what you expected or hoped to receive

---

Our Father in Heaven, praise be to Your name. The more I get to know You, the more I understand Your ways. The surprise of having a child at forty-one seems more than I could handle. You knew I could handle it and even used it as a tool to lead me further into Your purpose for my life. Most of the time, I look for things to play out according to my plan. Help me to visualize Your plan and purpose.

I need Your help in setting up boundaries for myself and my family. It is quite evident that we can't always say "yes." May I be guided by You, leaning not to my own ways. I'm learning to stop, look and listen when I see red flags in my mind. I thank You for always looking out for me even when I make wrong choices. In your Son's Name, Amen.

Chapter 12

Bend the Rules

When you've hit a brick wall call mother! ~ Sharon Lebsack

Lee's best friend, Jerry Spain, whom he grew up with as a boy, was his roommate in college and is his lifelong friend. He became instrumental in Lee's interest in the continent of Africa. Jerry accepted the call to East Africa as a missionary a few years after college graduation. At first, Jerry's wife, Joy, didn't hear this call but was willing to follow her husband because she believed in his calling. As the years unfolded, Joy was very comfortable and effective as a missionary. Jerry invited Lee to bring some men from our church to assist in building a church in Kenya, East Africa. Lee spoke in several churches, along with holding crusades, and soon developed a burden for the lost and dying in this country. African people were so open and longing for answers to their needs of impoverishment.

We came back several times to hold crusades in villages and towns where a church was to be "planted." Lee took the music team from our church, as well as others who wanted to experience a mission trip. We would be in crusades for a total of three weeks at a time. Lee and I, and sometimes our girls, were part of the music team.

Our girls began using their musical talents in singing with us as a family. The girls learned to sing parts (soprano, mezzo-soprano, and contralto) with Lee and me in church, school, or in the car. Singing became another opportunity to bond together as a family. Piano, voice, and clarinet evolved as part of their musical backgrounds.

Posters and banners would be placed all over the villages and countryside with as many as 10,000 African people walking and riding bikes to hear the music, along with the Word of God. Thousands would come forward to accept Christ as their personal Savior. Lee ministered to their hearts. At first, my heart was not in these trips, but as we saw results in these meetings, I started believing that I was intended to be part of this outreach. There were times that we would go door-to-door inviting people to the meetings. I had many opportunities to speak with the wives of missionaries and others in leadership programs.

These crusades were scheduled months ahead of time and one of the trips was scheduled in November of 1979. In my mind, there was no thought of taking a baby on this trip. I would not be going. A three-month-old, nursing baby was enough reason for me to stay home.

One night Lee addressed the subject and I could not believe he expected me to go. "We need you on the music team, Sharon, and you are also scheduled to speak to the missionary wives."

"I'm not going!" Our discussions and disagreements were held in soft voices learned from our days of staying in the homes of other families. Further, we did not want our girls hearing loud, angry voices. We spoke loud with our eyes and the soft-spoken word. My mind was made up and no one was going to change it. I had no intention of taking our baby on this mission trip. Pastor's wife or not, my mind was made up on this occasion.

By now, Lee knew I was a fairly submissive wife and most of the time adjusted to his way of thinking, but if I felt very strongly about something I could be very stubborn. I was definitely in a stubborn mode and was determined I was not going to change my mind about this trip. So what was a man to do when his wife would not change her mind about something so very important? Maybe call her mother for some maternal persuasion? While pouting in my bedroom, I heard Lee call out my name.

"Sharon, It's your mother." Without my knowing about it, Lee called my mother, who loved him like a son.

I had no idea what she was about to say. "Sharon, Lee called me and explained your situation about going to Africa. He said you are refusing to go, and this would definitely impact the effectiveness of the team. Since this event was scheduled before Tiffany was expected, I think you should reconsider your decision. Tiffany will be fine. If Lee's parents would come and take care of her, would that help change your decision?"

I loved my mom, her judgment had always been well thought out. Praying before speaking and acting was at the top of her list. I did not say a word for a few seconds and then answered, "It will be so hard to leave Tiffany, but if Lee's parents can come to stay with the baby I guess I can consider it."

Lee stood in the open door smiling. I told him I had other considerations. I would go if we talk with the pediatrician and our counselor friend, Dr. Richard Dobbins. I wanted their opinion of a three-week separation of mother and baby. He would then call his parents to ask if they would agree to come for three weeks to take care of their three-month-old, nursing granddaughter. If all of this was positive, I would go, but still did not want to. Of course, I had to add that as the last word.

The next day I called our pediatrician and then Dr. Dobbins. To my surprise, they both said the baby would be fine under these circumstances. They added to their assessment that "the mother," being me, would have to cope with the emotional and physical separation. Lee called his parents and they were willing to come for three weeks to take care of their grandchild. Tami and Tonya would be going with us on this trip, so grandma and grandpa would be able to completely devote their time to baby Tiffany.

Homesickness was my middle name while on this trip. I asked to hold every little African baby that came close to me. During the day, I kept to myself as much as possible, on the verge of crying most of the time. This was something different for me. I had, over the years, learned to bury my feelings—a learned behavior of keeping my feelings under control. As a pastor's wife, I always found a replacement for emotional outbreaks and everything would be fine. It was good that I faced the reality of this mission trip while giving myself permission to grieve separation. Each night of the crusade, I was at peace because I knew this was where I was supposed to be.

As I spoke to the missionary wives I told them the story of leaving my three-month-old baby for three weeks, explaining that this was not my plan, but God's. My intent was not to garner their pity for me, but I truly believed God planned for me to come to Africa, to encourage each of them. God cared that much about each of them and saw their sacrifices for His work. Their testimonies surprised me. With tears in their eyes, they put into words how elated they were that I would leave the comforts of home and willingly come to bring words of hope, encouragement, and consolation to them. They sometimes felt God had forsaken them and found it difficult to stay in this faraway country.

It was a stretch hearing the phrase "willingly come" since I had not been willing until God dealt strongly with me through my mother. Hearing His voice, listening to His voice, and acting on His calling brings fulfillment.

BACK HOME

Exhausted, but elated by God's power, we arrived at the South Bend airport, made the last leg of our trip by bus, and pulled into the church parking lot to find one of our board members waiting. He pulled Lee aside and shared some sad news about Teddy, our dog. Tonya's special dog, old and blind, had fallen into our pool and died. Lee took Tonya aside and shared the news. We didn't want her going home expecting her little dog to welcome her back. As tears filled her eyes, her daddy told her we would get another dog.

When we pulled up to our home, I became a wonder woman —pushing open doors, running upstairs two steps at a time, while bolting into Tiffany's room. She looked at me with wide-eyes from her crib and smiled. Oh, what a relief it is! She still knows me. Thank you, God, and Grandma and Grandpa Lebsack. I think they were saying the same words, Oh, what a relief it is!

Getting back into a normal routine became impossible. There is no normal in this profession. Lee was in the midst of building a Family Life Center which would be a combination of a gymnasium, fellowship hall, and counseling center. He also had to interview different people to be head of the counseling center.

A church full of young couples and new converts oftentimes carried a lot of baggage that needed to be dealt with under Christian influence. The counselors provided comfort, support, and direction to members of our congregation.

As Lee had been working on the counseling center, I concentrated on transitioning my outreaches. The following verse became a regular prayer for me.

Search me, God, and know my heart; test me and know my anxious thoughts. Psalm 139:23 [NIV]

I knew that God developed my gifts for this specific time in my life. It was different, uncertain, unfamiliar, new, exciting, and much more. I felt everything in my life now worked in preparing me for my specific purpose.

As people came for counseling, we found there were various needs: those who needed mentoring or coaching, those who needed spiritual counsel, and some who had weighty issues to deal with in life. Our director asked if I would have time once a week to help interview new clients. I thought I would feel comfortable doing this and found when God was asking me to sacrifice for Him, He gave me the strength and time to accomplish His work.

Life was busy but purposeful and fulfilling. Tami was in her second year of college and Tonya was a junior in high school. Most of us in our family were playing tennis, while Tonya especially excelled. She became ranked in our region and later received a college scholarship. I continued playing tennis and started taking golf lessons. We found a key to good family health—stay together, pray together, and play together.

INTERESTING TIDBITS

I was always very cautious in putting myself out there as a confidant to the women of our church. Needy, exasperating, and clingy, many women always need someone to talk to and who better to talk to than the pastor's wife? I set boundaries out of fear of becoming too involved or exploited. I learned my lesson at different times.

One day a young woman in her twenties asked if I could meet her to talk about her life. I happened to be free and set up a time, she told me she would come by and pick me up. I hesitated because I wanted to make her feel accepted. Reluctantly, I agreed and that turned out to be the wrong decision.

When I got in her car, a strange sensation crept up my spine and I asked, "Where are we going."

"Oh, let's just drive around," she said.

I got very quiet. My spirit sensed something was wrong.

"I've been living the life of a lesbian," she confessed. "What do you think of that?"

"Well, God loves everyone and died on the cross for all."

"I'm not going to take you home, Sharon." She flashed me a strange smile.

Immediately, my spirit called out to God. Boldness rose up inside me. "Let me out! Drop me off right now and I will walk."

"I was just kidding." Her smile faded.

"Take me home!" I felt God's hand in this meeting in spite of the circumstances. The young woman did as I requested and not another word was said. She continued attending the church. Lee and I prayed for her, however, my boundaries became mandatory.

***

Another time, a lady from our church called me on the phone and asked if she could come over for some spiritual counsel and prayer. I felt apprehensive about this, but I couldn't process the ramifications fast enough to tell her no. Other people can come up with a good refusal immediately. Perhaps I would overthink not wanting to hurt anyone's feelings (Lee has coached me on having phrases in my mind for such times as this.)

Tiffany was home at the time and I had a feeling this might be a very strange meeting. I set Tiffany up out in our yard with some games and snacks and explained that she needed to stay out here while I talked with a lady. The doorbell rang and the lady was smiling, this was a good sign. We sat down at our kitchen table, as she proceeded to tell of her fears and thoughts.

"Sharon, pray for me. I feel like I might be demon-possessed."

My heart raced. *Okay, God. Why did I open my home to this? We should have met at the church. Lord, my child is here and who knows where this is going to lead.*

As the woman continued telling me of voices and strange things happening in her house. I made a promise to never get caught in a position like this again.

All at once she said, "Where is your restroom? I'm getting sick and it could be that demon."

Immediately, I showed her to our guest bathroom. She shut the door. Gagging and vomiting sounds erupted from the space.. My heart pounded in my chest as I hurried to get a towel in case she had to wash up.

"I feel so much better now," she said as she opened the bathroom door.

"I'm glad you are feeling better. Let's pray."

I prayed, praising God for this woman's deliverance and asked the Holy Spirit to be with her as she walked in faith and obedience to become the woman God created her to be. After prayer, she thanked me and left.

She was on my mind as I rushed to the next commitment. When there are a thousand people or more in your congregation, there's always something happening. Lee and I both made an effort to enjoy people outside our congregation, too. We found this variation good for us. We enjoyed a balance of church and community.

Our neighbors across the street moved to South Bend from New York and were anxious to meet new people. They invited us over for a delightful meal. Our girls were invited and Tami was asked to be their "exclusive babysitter." Meeting people from other walks of life intrigued us. Of course, we knew we wanted to reciprocate. As busy as we were, we thought we found an evening that would work into our schedule.

Since it was summertime, I made my suggestion to Lee. "Let's invite our neighbors over for homemade ice cream and chocolate chip cookies. The kids can go swimming. We adults can visit and then have our ice cream and cookies." He thought this was a great idea. I called our neighbors, giving them an invite to our home for ice cream and cookies around 7:30. I went on to suggest our children could go swimming while we adults would visit and then we all could have our homemade ice cream and cookies. After thinking about it, I should have invited them for dessert, instead of making the assumption that they would come after dinner.

The day they were to come over happened to be cloudy and rainy. The first indication that there was a misunderstanding appeared when we met them at the door. They presented me with a box of candy saying, "This is for the chef!" Well, that part went right over my head until later in the evening. The plan was for the kids to play ping pong and games in our finished basement. I made up some little snacks: chips, pretzels, and pop. We adults could sit in the family room getting to know a little more about each of our lives, then serve dessert about 8:30 or 9:00.

About 8:45. I went down to see if the kids were out of snacks and the little girl said, "We don't want to eat any more or we will spoil our dinner."

What! They were here for a meal and what we had was homemade ice cream and cookies. I hurried upstairs and asked Lee to come into the kitchen, as I relayed the latest news.

"Our neighbors are here for dinner and we have nothing. I'm calling Pizza Hut. Run down and bring it back quickly."

Meantime, Lee asked Tami if she could entertain them with some of the readings she had been practicing. Of course, she was thrilled. I made a salad, got the table set and Lee got back with pizza. We told them we thought since this was a family gathering we would just have pizza and then homemade ice cream and cookies. They were thrilled. After they left, Lee and I laughed so hard, we practically rolled on the floor. Did we pull it off? We will never know. Now the phrase "This is for the chef" made sense.

On one particular Sunday morning, we had an exceptionally large crowd at church. The ushers helped the overflow of people find seats. Lee sat on the platform, anticipating stepping to the pulpit to deliver the sermon when he saw an incident which brought him to full stance.

Marion, an elderly, special-needs lady in our church always sat in the same seat. Today, someone was sitting in "Marion's Seat." She walked to "her" regular seat, took her purse and hit the man in the head with a loud explanation, "This is my seat!"

Lee immediately sent one of the pastors down to try to intervene, but it was too late, the couple left. We all understood Marion's child-like ways and remembered what Jesus said.

Jesus said, "Let the little children come to me, and do not hinder them, for the kingdom of heaven belongs to such as these." Matthew 19:14 [NIV]

When working with hundreds and thousands of people you will have many happy, sad, and interesting stories. Some incidents can be very disturbing. Early one Monday morning, a stranger met Lee in the parking lot of our church. The man was very friendly and shook hands with Lee.

"I've heard great things about this church. I'm very interested in missions and am planning on a trip, but need more financing."

Lee listened to him and replied, "We only give through our denomination and our missions budget is full now."

The man became quite defensive and said to Lee, "I do not understand. God called me and you're missing a great opportunity to be part of my mission trip." The man's anger grew as he continued threatening, "You just watch, bad things are going to start happening to you and your family."

When Lee got home that night, he told me about the incident. We weren't really concerned.

Several weeks passed and unexplained things happened to our family. Lee drove his car through the garage one day without opening the door (Well, that was funny.) The girls seemed to frequently be sick. Then my mammogram test revealed a lump. It was serious enough for the doctor to meet with Lee and me concerning the "C" word. Lee and I became anxious.

One morning, Lee and I addressed these strange happenings. This man had threatened our family and proclaimed evil over us. We knew we were covered with the blood of Christ, but our lives were being affected. I called my mother and asked what she thought. She didn't hesitate at all in giving spiritual counsel.

"Sharon, this can be very real and you need to bring together the elders of the church and have them anoint you and Lee with oil. Rebuke this threat!"

Knowing there is much evil in this world, we did this in short order. Immediately, we saw a change in the pattern of bad things happening in our family.

A few weeks later, a couple of miles from our home, a minister and his wife were murdered in their bed. Coincidence?

What a sad outcome for our community. Could that have been us?

I never sat in the same place during our services. I had watched pastors' wives down through the years always sit at the same "designated" seat. I felt self-conscious about people in the congregation scrutinizing their pastor's wife. *What was I wearing? Did I have a smile on my face?* I sat with different people every service. I never thought anything about it as I had always done this and it felt like the right thing for me.

One day, while walking down the aisle, I noticed Dorothy, a single grandmother who was raising her grandchildren, sitting all alone. I decided Dorothy would be the one I would sit with on that day. She looked at me with big eyes and said, "You are sitting with me?" I said, "Yes, I am, Dorothy. You are special." Tears welled up in her eyes and she shared a little about herself before the service started. She mentioned her husband was in prison for murder, plus her son was also in prison. She was raising her grandchildren.

My heart went out to her like I had never felt before. Dorothy had found Jesus Christ during the time of her husband's trial and had been living for Him, bringing her grandchildren to church ever since. She asked me a question, "Sharon, would you ever come to my home so I could tell you my story in full?" I answered her without hesitation, "Yes, we will set up a time and I will come to your home." We set a time and I went to Dorothy's humble home to hear the story of her life. I will never forget Dorothy and her dedication, commitment, and faith. Her little granddaughter and Tiffany met and became friends.

Thank you, God, for putting it in my heart to sit with different people every Sunday so I can get a true understanding of the people in our congregation. I love these people!

In all of our churches, the demographics would range from poor and needy to wealthy and affluent. The major part of our congregations was generally between twenty and fifty years of age. Young families with children are the heart of a church, especially where there's the OK (older kids) there to support, mentor, love, and pray (most of the time).

We had been asked out to dinner several times by one of the underprivileged young couples. They had a baby and lived in an old upstairs apartment. We felt apprehensive about going but did not want to make them feel bad, so we ultimately set a date that worked for everyone.

As the lady of the house put the final touches on our meal of spaghetti, she said, "Sharon, we are so happy you cared enough about us to come to our home for dinner. I decided to have spaghetti but did not have a pan big enough to cook it in. We did not have money to purchase a pan and I don't know the people in this apartment building well enough to ask to borrow. I did the next best thing. I looked around the house and decided the metal diaper pail would work. Of course, I had to wash the diapers."

Lord, did I misunderstand? Are we going to be eating food cooked in a used diaper pail? Jesus, please help us!

I decided not to tell Lee and just trust God. This precious

family was offering us the best of what they had available. We ate the spaghetti dinner cooked in the diaper pail.

Father: If You had shown me what was ahead of me in life, I think I would have thought that life belonged to another. Things are happening so fast that I don't have time to doubt You or myself. When I do, You are always there with words of encouragement and instructions from the Book that was written for me from the beginning of time. All I can say is, "Thank You" for trusting me with the life You've planned. In the name of Your Son. Amen.

Chapter 13

Love Unbending

"He's still working on Me." ~ Sharon Lebsack

After close to twenty-five years in ministry, we understood God's purpose—saw His vision, trained people for ministry and help them advance toward their goals. We realized that not all of our congregation would agree with the vision the leadership had for the church or the city. Music had become a wonderful part of the worship time. But here again, the senior adult part of our congregation was still hanging on to the old hymns. Now there is nothing wrong with the old hymns. They are wonderful, but the younger part of our congregation loved the new songs that drew them into the worship service.

It seemed that most disgruntled people have some deep-seated issues. Sometimes loving them was a WWJD (What Would Jesus Do) situation and worked most of the time. Many unhappy people felt they must voice their complaints to other members. However, it seemed that these issues would frequently end up with the pastor's wife.

I always wanted to fix problems and try to explain to Lee what he might do to make them happier. In fact, there were times I acted as if I was his "personal" Holy Spirit, even though the real Holy Spirit would do a much better job of speaking to his heart, and the problem would be truly fixed.

Lee's way was to stay with the leadership and the majority of the church while continuing to press forward. Satan has a way of trying to get our minds off of the real objective of winning souls. We always worked tirelessly to have a group or program for everyone in every age group.

I had learned from my mother that some people would try to sow discord by calling prayer meetings or other meetings to discuss their agenda against the pastor or leadership. It is not the pastor or his wife's place to become involved in these matters of discontent. The Bible is quite clear regarding when there is an issue with those in authority or leadership, pray about it then go to discuss it directly with the individual.

During a period toward the end of our time in South Bend, a group of about twenty people called a private meeting to discuss their concerns about how their tithe was being spent and that they didn't like the emphasis on the younger families. Tami and Tonya got word of this meeting and, on their own, decided to show up. They met in a room at church, so the girls went straight up to the front row and sat listening to this group's issues. We had no idea the girls were going, but they were there to protect their father's reputation. This made me so sad because we had always tried to shield our girls from any remarks or criticism from church members.

Pride and power struggles go way back to the Bible days. There are people today in our churches challenging authority of the leadership as in days of old. Sometimes it comes from a staff member or maybe a longtime member who wants to retain power in the church and can't or won't submit to the authority of a pastor, the elders, or the church board. Power can destroy or create.

Lee and I have noticed down through the years if things like this raise their ugly heads, God will allow these situations to get our attention. South Bend church was definitely in God's plan for our family. We will always thank God for the many souls who found Jesus Christ as their personal Savior. God used the twelve years of our ministry there to continue leadership growth in our lives. God took this time through circumstances to get my attention to hear His voice.

BUT I WANT EVERYONE TO LIKE ME!

I found out a long time ago that trying to make people like me is hard work. Dr. Richard Dobbins (founder and CEO of Emerge Ministries) said one time, "I couldn't believe that there were some people who just didn't like me. I was a good person and was working so hard to shepherd and help people." He went on to say, "There will always be a percentage of people who just don't like you, whether it's your personality, something you said, an action, a look, or just a feeling." So the quicker we come to that conclusion, the quicker we can go on with life.

Almost everybody has experienced some type of rejection at one time or another. You do not have to come from a dysfunctional or abusive background to experience rejection. Let's be honest, REJECTION HURTS! We can feel rejection by a look or a word, and then we ASSUME the rest. Once we stop caring so much what people think of us, the quicker we get over that feeling of rejection. The Bible says:

If God be for us (me), who can be against us (me)? Romans 8:31[KJV]

Rejection is one of Satan's favorite tools for women in general, but especially for WIM (women in ministry). In my younger years, a rejection of me or my spouse would throw me right into a feeling of worthlessness. We can go from worthlessness into self-pity, self-pity into anger, and anger into depression. Not a good place to be! Sometimes we catch ourselves before it's too late, other times we just let ourselves go. The sad note is taking ownership of that rejection and then actually rejecting ourselves.

The answer, of course, is found in the Word of God. If you are rooted in acceptance and love, then you will develop good things in your life—things like self-control, meekness, faithfulness, goodness, kindness, patience, peace, joy, and love. Start allowing God to do a work in you in building your security in Him.

Do you get your "fixes" from people, from your spouse, from things? It doesn't work! If you are depending on someone else to meet all of your needs, it doesn't work. Once I learned that lesson, the load lightened. It didn't hurt when it didn't happen. Oh sure, we may still feel a tinge now and then of rejection, but downplay it. We need to learn to be connected so close to God the Father that He becomes the **source** for every rejection and unmet need in our lives.

"No weapon formed against you shall prosper,
And every tongue which rises against you in judgment
You shall condemn.
This is the heritage of the servants of the LORD,
And their righteousness is from Me,"
Says the LORD.
Isaiah 54:17 [NKJV]

GROWING UP

Our girls spent all of their teenage years in South Bend. Tami graduated from high school and chose to attend North Central Bible College in Minneapolis, Minnesota. Her high school sweetheart, John Bullard, was attending this school. A third-generation member of our church, John became Tami's choice young man to marry. That made us very happy. By now, Tami and John both knew they had a call of God upon their lives for ministry. John was four years older than Tami. They married in June of the year he graduated. John accepted a position of youth pastor in a church. They stayed there for two years.

Lee then invited John to come to our South Bend church to serve as our youth pastor. Soon, Lee asked Tami to be his personal secretary. This worked great as he could train her to be the best and that he did. We were thrilled to have Tami and

John on our staff. Lee mentored John, and Tami got to see firsthand what being a pastor's wife was really like. Even though she had grown up in our home, many issues weren't always evident. We shielded our daughters from the hard challenges within the structure of the church.

Tami and John were learning the various aspects of ministry. South Bend was the church where they had grown up. It isn't always easy to come back to your home church as a staff member. There were times of discouragement, but, little-by-little, the transition became smooth. Our first granddaughter, Krystal, was born in South Bend. Lee and I were parents of a five-year-old and now grandparents of this precious gift.

When Tonya was 15, she made a list of four boys in our church whom she thought she might like to go out with. Tami instructed her younger sister on how to "flirt" with the one she wanted to date the most. Tonya, strong and committed in everything she did as a child and teenager, had many friends but usually developed one or two lifetime and loyal ones. Our paperboy, Mark Myers, was also from a third-generation family in our church. Number one on her list, Mark was invited to Tonya's boy and girl party. She felt very hesitant about a boy and girl party, but her big sister talked her into having one. Of course, the four boys on her list were among the invitees. We learned later that Mark didn't want to come to the party, but his father told him if he was invited to the pastor's home, it was his duty to go.

Mark and Tonya really hit it off. Mark, one year older than Tonya, went to college the next year. When Tonya graduated from high school, she received a tennis scholarship to Evangel University in Springfield, Missouri. Mark also decided to go there his second year. After one year at Evangel, Mark and Tonya were ready for marriage. Mark had two more years before he would earn his degree from Indiana University. They were a happy couple, living back home in South Bend where our second granddaughter, Kayla, was born. Another joy!

Tiffany attended our church school, sang in our children's choir, loved being in charge, and took control wherever she went. This was a child with a cause and a solution. She planned all of her birthday parties. We paid for prizes and made the cake. When Tiffany was eight, we had an evangelist come to our church. He told the story about going to an orphanage where he prayed for the children to have faith and to pray for other children when they had needs. Tiffany wanted him to pray for her, which he did.

One Sunday our family gathered at our home for a meal. Tiffany and our three year-old-granddaughter, Krystal, left the table heading back to Tiffany's room to play. After clearing the table, Tami and I headed back to check on the girls. Krystal, suffered asthma attacks from the time she was a baby, and we were always watchful. What we saw taking place amazed us. Ten year-old-Tiffany leaned over Krystal and prayed for her to be healed. Krystal never had another asthma attack.

We knew Tiffany would be a leader wherever God led her in life. She didn't realize that an abrupt change would be coming into her life. She was a lighthearted child and loved life. She would sing at the top of her lungs in the shower. That old song kept coming up... "There's a change made since I've been born again."

We are blessed if we do right in the sight of God.

Whenever I ran into a brick wall, I found if I searched for a scripture that men and women of God used when they came to a standstill, it would work for me. In Chronicles, the writer uses the word "seek" twenty-nine times—urging those wanting to please God to earnestly desire the Lord's presence, fellowship, kingdom, and holiness.

Seeking the Lord involves:

1. Turn to the Lord with your whole heart.
2. Hunger for righteousness.
3. Commit yourself to God's will.
4. Rely on God to be your ultimate helper.
5. **My plan to review Asa's plan:**
6. Ask God for help - 2 Chronicles 14:11
7. If you seek you will find - 2 Chronicles 15:1-2
8. In distress, turn to God – 2 Chronicles 15:4
9. Be strong and don't give up. – 2 Chronicles 15:7 C
10. Cleanse yourself from sin. – 2 Chronicles 15:8
11. Build an altar and pray. – 2 Chronicles 15:8
12. Assemble yourselves together. – 2 Chronicles 15:10
13. Enter into a covenant to seek the Lord with all your

heart and soul. - 2 Chronicles 15:12

14. Shout and give praise with rejoicing. – 2 Chronicles 15:14

15. Continue to seek God eagerly and He will be found. – 2 Chronicles 15:15

16. Give to the Lord. – 2 Chronicles 15:18

God gives direction.

As Lee and I sought the Lord, we felt in our heart that God was calling us to a change in our ministry. We needed time to seek to do right in the sight of God. Lee felt the Lord had lifted the burden of the South Bend church and knew there was something else on the horizon. He had been feeling a call in his heart to raise funds for the Continent of Africa. He resigned as pastor of the church and gained financial support for our Africa mission projects. The result was, we did not have to take funding from offerings taken for the projects. We felt that this was God's plan because doors kept opening.

Within a couple of weeks, Lee had services scheduled across the country for the next twelve months. Before He started this schedule of raising funds for our Africa project, we felt we needed a sabbatical. For the next three months, we took this time for rest and renewal.

I had talked with pastors' wives in various states and situations who were not always in agreement with their husband when he felt a new challenge. Some didn't want to leave the comfort of where they were, while others did not have the same call as their husbands. I remember one pastor's wife in particular who had such a burden for missions, but her husband did not. If my opinion was sought, I always advised the couple to pray and work together until a compromise was made that brought them to a satisfactory agreement. While some had such a division that their marriage suffered, there are those who actually ended their marriage because they couldn't come to an agreement. There is always a solution for things such as this and discord is not an answer.

As a pastor's wife, I had always told myself I didn't have a call to the ministry, but I had a call to be a helpmate to my husband and a mother to my children. After years of seeking fulfillment, I came to the conclusion we are ALL called. We answer that call every day of our lives. God's plan and purpose are for us to have fellowship with Him, with one another in encouragement, prayer, and love. So do I have a call? Yes, I do! Consequently, wherever our family may be led, I will work in my calling and purpose to women all over the world.

Lee would have to spend quite a bit of time in Africa. I trusted him to do the right thing, even though I had doubts about this being best for our family. Our sabbatical was not only for rest but also for God to put His plan into play. Lee and I used this time to work through the questions. Security is always of utmost importance to us as women, and this became part of my concern. During this time, Lee received several phone calls from a church in Dallas, Texas, wanting him to consider being their pastor.

One of the last Sundays in South Bend came to my mind. My mother was living in her own home in South Bend at the age of eighty-five. She rarely missed church, but this particular Sunday she was not feeling well and stayed home. The worship team was singing a song before the message, while Lee was on the platform with a mint in his mouth, preparing to speak. He started choking and unable to get his breath. He turned around toward the large cross at the back of the platform, praying to God. He was frantic until a peace came down and he caught his breath. He delivered the sermon with a great anointing.

On my way home after church, I stopped by to see how my mother was doing. As soon as I entered her home she exclaimed, "Is Lee okay?"

"Why do you ask?" I gave her a hug and followed her into the family room.

"Well, I was sitting in my comfy chair and all of a sudden I felt a great burden for Lee. Something very bad was happening." Mom stood and walked as if reenacting the scene. "As I walked around, I felt the Holy Spirit urging me to get a pen and paper. So I sat down at the kitchen table and started writing." Mom began to give me the general message. "Lee had been obedient to God, had seen great things in his ministry and God was going to do greater things than ever."

I took her hands and told her of his choking incident. "He was unable to catch his breath," my own breathing shuddered. "But then, peace came over him." I smiled, blinking back my emotions. "Then he delivered the message God had given him."

This was another confirmation that God was in control. It comforted us greatly." We both felt a release from the church in

South Bend. We left with great memories and learned many lessons. At the age of fifty, we felt confident in our leadership abilities. I had developed new gifts and knew God had a place for me as a woman who loved God. It was sad to leave the rest of our family, but God had plans for their lives too.

After several weeks and many calls from a Dallas church, we were both in agreement that we should make a trip to Dallas to check out this opportunity.

Changes would divide our family geographically. Tonya, Mark, and Kayla, our new grandchild, stayed in South Bend while Mark finished his senior year at Indiana University. Tami and John accepted their first position as lead pastor in Michigan.

I would miss our daughters as they were my best friends. It's very hard for a pastor's wife to have a best friend. So my adult daughters were my "besties." Those grandbabies were very special. I saw them several times a week. Now, I would be leaving part of my heart. But God had given me Tiffany. He knew what He was doing all the time.

Dear Father in Heaven, You always know what You're doing in spite of us, Your children, trying to help You out. Thank You for always understanding we're just human. From the beginning of our ministry, You have led, directed, and counseled us every step of the way. Our children have survived as PKs (Preacher's Kids). Thank You for opening doors for our children. Bless our coming move. Tiffany will not want to leave South Bend, but from past experiences I know, You always come through when we are obedient. I praise Your name above all names. In everything we say and do, we glorify Your name. In Jesus' name, Amen.

Sharon Lebsack

Part Four
Dallas, Texas

Welcome to Texas, y'all! Gimme a hug!

Chapter 14

Destination Dallas

For such a time as this. ~ God

Refreshed, we left South Bend, Indiana, with a feeling God had prepared and tested us for our upcoming ministry in Dallas. We stepped into the warm, sunny Texas weather and dove into southern hospitality. As soon as we drove into the larger-than-life city of Dallas, we felt at home. God let us both know this was His plan.

Lee and I had voiced our dreams of living in the South. The clear skies with the sun shining every day. It felt like a vacation. Again, God had heard our small desire because, for the past twelve years, we lived with many cloudy days, snow, rain, and always cold.

"When God is in it, everything will be perfect," I remembered the phrase from a minister friend. Perfect would be awesome. However, just because it is God's perfect plan doesn't mean we'll like it or think it's perfect. We expected this new beginning to be similar to our early days in South Bend: exuberant welcomes, excitement, happiness, and a willingness to do

whatever to join Lee in finding God's vision for that city. Ten-year-old Tiffany sat in the back seat of our car reading a book. This was her first trip to Dallas. From time to time, sighs came from the backseat as Tiffany emoted her unhappiness about leaving her friends, school, and church. We just knew when she saw Dallas all of this would change.

"Tiffany," Lee said in his fatherly voice, "Look at the beautiful skyline of our new city."

Back seat silence answered. Then Tiffany mumbled, "This is not **my** new city. I want to go back to South Bend." This gave us quite an indication of the challenge we faced with our daughter.

The atmosphere of driving through the city changed as our Tiffany displayed her disappointment. We approached Carrollton and soon caught sight of our new, beautiful home, with wonderful landscaping and a backyard playground. The movers were already there, buzzing in and out the front door.

"Tiffany," Lee used his cherry father voice, "Let's go around to the backyard."

As she followed him, she stopped in her tracks, smiled and said, "A pool? Yaaaay!"

At last, we saw a smile, which gave us some hope. A large basketball court came into view and now, Lee was smiling.

We worried a bit about Tiffany acclimating to the move but knew God had a plan. The teacher of the Wednesday night girl's program at the church, called to tell me they were going to have a welcome party for Tiffany. I wanted this to be a surprise for her; therefore we didn't tell her about the party.

Then our first week in our new home, the director of the

girl's program called to tell me there wouldn't be a welcome party for Tiffany. The committee thought this unfair; unless they had a welcome party for every little girl's first time. My heart sank, but I was so thankful I had not shared the first invitation with Tiffany.

This book may be about a pastor's wife, however, it might be more appropriately named, *Confessions of a Pastor's Family*. The preacher's kids (PKs) have a much more difficult journey of adjustment. Moved around like checkers on a board, they walk the "between" line. Not getting too much special treatment and yet they are treated special and judged because they are the PK. They must smile, but not too much, be friendly but guarded. The list is endless. The only way a mom can endure this stress on her family is to know God doesn't have grandchildren. He is there for my children just as He is for me.

Coming to a mega city like Dallas was as thrilling as going on a roller coaster. The anticipation of sharing with other churches to further Christianity in (now) our town was monumental. The church was a beautiful, cathedral type, tall steeple, brick building with stained glass windows.

Our first Sunday proved to be very pleasant. The Southern hospitality was quite a change coming from the Mid-west. I just loved being smiled at, hugged, spoken to with that Southern charm. It seemed God had hand-picked several families in the church to take us under their wings for the transition. They recommended doctors, dentists, grocery stores, restaurants, and yes, even the best malls in Dallas. These couples will have many jewels in their crowns for their love and support. God Bless them from my heart! The leadership welcomed us, along with different individuals in the congregation. We had a reception after the Sunday night service to meet the members, and too soon I felt surveyed, scanned and checked over more than usual.

One man said, "Why did we have to get a Yankee for our pastor?" At the time, it felt like he really meant it, but then again we were new and didn't know the Dallas humor yet. We grew to love him.

In our former churches, the congregation had been thrilled to have new leadership so their vision could go forward. This time there seemed to be a comfort level of satisfaction with the old.

The good news in Dallas was I saw a vision for myself. God led me to my purpose—a purpose for this new season of my life. I have never been fearful of change and knew this could be good. Getting our new home settled and decorated to my liking kept me busy.

However, life threw Tiffany a huge curve. She had always been in our Christian school, so the idea of going to public school in the fourth grade upset her. I felt sorry for her. This change stretched her way beyond her comfort zone. She had been outgoing, now she became introverted. Her teacher shared with us how Tiffany would go off by herself at recess to read a book. At home, she would practice piano for hours, read and study more than usual.

One time, I asked, "Tiffany, don't you think you've practiced long enough?" What mother would ever have to say this to her child? Me!

Tiffany's normal singing-in-the-shower sessions stopped. Faced with the changes in our lives, we had to work through the ramifications of our big move. After a year, we were able to enroll her in a Christian school, which turned out to be another life change for Tiffany. She loved it and once again, blossomed.

God worked it out for her best.

Changes proved difficult for me too. I was now just an "attendee" not a member of the staff. Feelings of not fitting in snuck up on me and took root. Even though I complained about being "volunteered" by Lee to so many different positions in our former churches, this was way on the other side of the spectrum. Was there a balance somewhere? I decided to work at finding it. Like Tiffany, I missed my best friends—our two adult daughters. We were close and had always shared life's challenges.

The family was expecting some exciting news, a new grandson. Caleb. Of course, Mama Kay, Papa, and Tiffany made a car trip from Dallas to Michigan to meet this new addition to our family. Being with Tami, John, and Krystal brought much joy in welcoming Caleb.

As the week drew to an end, we returned to Dallas to continue our conventional lifestyle. Oh, that's not true, let's use the word diverse, but exciting.

In a few days, I received a phone call from one of the women in our church. I remember meeting this lady who was quite talkative and welcoming. She was asking me to meet her for lunch. This could be good, I enjoyed getting to know our congregation in a more personal way.

"Sharon, my thoughts have been on you. I knew adjusting to a new place could be quite disconcerting." She went on to say, "If you ever need to talk to someone about your new adjustment, please feel free to share it with me. I will pray for you and it will be kept confidential. You can trust me."

This girl-talk over our new move, some of the challenges and changes, felt good. I had always been careful about talking about very personal subjects. In Dallas, I didn't have my grown-up daughters to share my problems, so this might turn out to be something good.

You might have guessed it. I soon found out this woman shared my feelings with some of her friends. I knew better than to discuss feelings with a member of the church, but I felt lonely. The incident didn't cause any problems, but a definite reminder of who I am—a "pastor's wife" whose life, feelings, thoughts, and dreams have to be exemplary.

Many times when a new pastor comes to a congregation, it is acceptable protocol for the staff to resign along with the resigning pastor. In this case, the church board made an exception and told Lee they had asked the whole staff to stay and work with him. This was fine with Lee because we had met the staff and gone out to dinner with them. We felt it would work and it did. This staff became very close to us, supportive, and went along with Lee's vision for the church. They helped us get around the city to hospitals, restaurants and anything else that we might need help in locating. Cell phones appeared about this time, so Lee made many calls to one of the staff members if he got lost or couldn't find his way. We were a team that God put together for this Dallas adventure.

It didn't take long for me to talk to the wives of staff members about getting together once a month for sharing, prayer and maybe going through a book together. They were all in agreement. First, we studied the book, *Tale of Three Kings* by Gene Edwards. We all faced similar issues as pastors' wives. This became a bonding, confidential time, a treasure—an area of ministry where I could feel connected. These precious wives were going through acute adjustments also, unsettling issues for us to face as pastor and pastor's wife.

The good news was Tonya and Mark were moving to Texas. Yea! Mark had a job opportunity. I would have two of my three daughters and, of course, our granddaughter. Kayla was the icing on the cake. About a year of getting settled in Dallas, the anticipation of more icing on the cake was evident. Justin was born, our fourth grandchild, and only true Texan.

Thinking about Life

Some days, I look up into the sky and see the sun, feel the warmth and know all is well. Other days, I look up into the sky and see the dark clouds and feel frightened of the coming storm. But God can make a difference if we will allow the tough times to teach, train and grow us as people. Can you imagine a difference it would make if we learned from our mistakes? It could start a chain reaction that grows from me, to you, to someone else. It might be difficult, but let's determine to make a difference by doing our small part—our link in the chain. God depends on us to reflect who He is.

Lee adjusted to the inherited staff, a staff who worked with him on the logistics of this Dallas church. Lee's vision has always been to reach the lost in our community along with growth in all areas of the Christian walk for the church. As the months passed, the circumstances of our church came into focus.

One segment of the congregation wanted to control the church. Some even came to Lee telling him what to preach or not to preach. This became quite an issue over time. All of the ministers on staff, along with their wives, supported, prayed, and encouraged each other. This bond gave us all a strength and steadfastness to keep going until there was unity at our church. If our pastor husbands were criticized or ostracized in any way, we became very protective.

Now, let's think about this and be cognizant of the facts. We, as wives, can criticize our husband but no one else can!

One Sunday a lady stood at the outside door of the church telling visitors they would not be happy with the pastor of this church.

*But God—do You really know what You're doing? Did You bring us to this city and church for such a time as **this**?*

God always knows what He's doing. We knew He had prepared, groomed, and taught us for this time in our lives. Over time, God had pruned our branches in order to see us flourish and bear fruit. All of those years when we thought it was challenging, God snipped, snipped, and pruned us for Dallas, Texas. God knew we were prepared.

On the outside, all looked well at this church and there were a lot of positives, but we soon found out the church had a history of a political battle. As long as there are people on this earth, there will be differences, struggles, and control issues. Trying to bring unity and peace anywhere is a huge challenge. But God reigns!

Even though the situation looked gloomy, we knew someone in Dallas, Texas, had been praying for God to send someone who would take this church to a new level.

For our struggle is not against flesh and blood, but against the rulers, against the authorities, against the powers of this dark world and against the spiritual forces of evil in the heavenly realms. Ephesians 6:12 [NIV]

Lee and I talked about the disruptive situations. After all, I am his co-pilot. Who else does he have to talk to? Who will share his innermost feelings? We did our talking away from the house on long walks. This gave us a two-fold solution. We didn't want Tiffany's young mind to be tainted by these challenges, plus we got away from phone calls.

Realizing Satan wanted to take charge of the Dallas church, we prepared for the release of that bondage. There was a night when I sat upright—out of a deep sleep. A large black cloud hovered over our bed. Immediately, I recognized this as "evil" and took authority over it.

"I rebuke you, Satan, in the name of Jesus! I plead the blood of Jesus over our home, this church, and this city." I watched the dark cloud float out of our room and our home, never to return. Looking back, I realized it was a warning from the Lord of the coming storm in the Dallas church.

My suggestion to everyone in and out of ministry is to take authority over evil. Recognize and know the power God has given you as a believer. Do not fear it, but know God stands by you as you demand Satan leave.

Taking Authority Over Satan

We have an instruction book (the Bible) giving us direction in taking authority over the evil powers. In dealing with people for years, especially from other non-Christian countries, we have been called for help in dealing with overcoming the powers of Satan.

- Demons are subject to God's name. Luke 10:17

- God has given us authority over the evil one. Luke 10:19

- In the name of Jesus, we have the power to cast out evil spirits. Mark 16:17

- Put on the full armor of God, so you can stand against

the devil. Ephesians 10-18

- Submit to God and resist the devil and he will flee from you. James 4:7

Pray in Jesus' name. Take authority by speaking forth over any evil spirits, commanding it in Jesus' name. Quote or read scripture. Study the Bible for direction. Do not fear.

That's what Jesus did and it's what He commanded His disciples to do. He cast out the demons and then ministered to the people. Because of the power of the Holy Spirit, we can do the same. We can cast out the evil and then love the one who channeled it.

The People in Your Life

1. You alone can make a difference as you look for the good in everyone.
2. There are at least two people in the world that you would die for.
3. At least 15 people in this world love you in some way.
4. The only reason anyone would ever hate you is that they want to be like you.
5. A smile from you can bring happiness to anyone, even if they don't like you.
6. Every night, someone thinks about you before they go to sleep.
7. You mean the world to someone.
8. You are special and unique.
9. Someone that you don't even know exists and loves you.

10. When you make the biggest mistake ever, something good comes from it.

11. When you think the world has turned its back on you take another look.

12. Always remember the compliments you received. Forget about the rude remarks.

(Sharon,) **Now what I am commanding you today is not too difficult for you or beyond your reach. Deuteronomy 30:11 [NIV]**

Dear Father in Heaven, how could it be that You have so much love for Your children? You gave Your only Son so that we might have the reality of a Savior. My life would be so empty without You. I confess I do not have all of the answers to life. There have been times I have prayed for an intervention but only felt silence. You have given us a mind and wisdom, if we seek it, to solve many of our actions. Sometimes we just can't do it alone. Thank You for always being there when I feel alone. Down through the years, I've learned You are usually never early, but never late. The big secret is You have all of the answers. Thank You for being You, and thank You for creating me with the hope of becoming like You. Amen.

Chapter 15

Real Friends or Not

"A good friend is like a four-leaf-clover—hard to find and lucky to have."
~An Irish Proverb

We received word that Tami, John, Krystal, and Caleb were moving to Texas. This news blessed me so much because our entire family would now be in one place, near me. My wish had been for all of our family to be in one place, attending church, having meals and fun together, and now we would. God once again gave me the desire of my heart.

During this time, church life seemed far from perfect. Don't get me wrong, we loved our church. However, there are no perfect churches, no perfect people, no perfect pastors, and no perfect pastors' wives. It is a fact!

Lee's positive sermons challenged the congregation, and we kept smiling, praying, and loving. *But, God, send change, please.*

It was definitely time for a change. We were drowning in discouragement, thinking maybe we were not the ones to bring a transformation to this church.

At one point, Lee called a couple of friends to see if they had any positions open in their businesses—to no avail. A couple of churches contacted Lee to see if he would consider coming for an interview for the lead pastor. Both times we had the interview, met with elders and leaders, but God kept bringing our hearts back to where He had brought us. We could not shake the feeling that this was exactly where God wanted our ministry. As Lee's wife, my heart hurt for him, and for a time, I experienced concern that it might not work out.

Then what? I guess other women feel the same about their husband's security in jobs. It is wrong, but we expect a Christian church or business to be different. It hurt, and for a while, I lost the joy of the Lord. After being in ministry for a good many years, I finally realized that people are people, whether they call themselves Christian or not. Many found the gem of practicing Christ-likeness, others just never saw the need to practice what God's Word commands.

So then, while we have opportunity, let us do well to all people, and especially to those who are of the household of the faith. Galatians 6:10 [NASB]

Disappointments

If we take ownership of our disappointments, we will miss all of God's blessings. I know there have been times I have become so disappointed that things didn't go my way that I failed to see God's perfect plan for my life. When I focus on *my way*, *my will* and *my wants*, I tend to block God out of my focus.

In *My Utmost for His Highest*, Oswald Chambers has pointed out that "The surf that distresses the ordinary swimmer produces in the surf-rider the super joy of going clean through it." Let us apply that to our own circumstances, these very things: tribulation and persecution produce in us the super joy. They are not things to fight. The saint never knows the joy of the Lord in spite of tribulation but because of it.

I started thinking of great men and women in the Bible who must have faced deep disappointments: Joseph, Moses, Abraham, Daniel, Mary, Elijah, and many more. They no doubt felt their dreams had been shattered, when all the time God was working on their behalf to bring about His perfect plan.

Have you become so disappointed that you've lost sight of God's plan? What can you do? Let go of your will and your disappointments.

- ✓ Study the word of God.
- ✓ Pray and ask God to forgive you for your wrong focus.
- ✓ Memorize God's promises that can help you believe.
- ✓ Find a trusting Christian friend who will encourage you.
- ✓ Start looking at your disappointments as stepping stones to God's blessings.

Soon after, someone recommended a book to Lee titled *Dying for Change* by Leith Anderson. We both read the book. Lee then had his staff, elders, and board members read it. Then he bought books for every family in the church to read. Our home-study groups discussed the book. The message in the book spoke to everyone in an amazing way. The fact God could use something as small as a book to motivate change astonished me. It didn't take a big event, conference, or gathering.

After most of the leadership, staff, and congregation read *Dying for Change*, it became evident that this congregation was not reaching its present community. Some of the factors in the church did not want to change or go forward. Sometimes we get so satisfied in a comfortable state that it's hard to move. Leadership and staff realized it was time for the church to physically move the church to the northern suburbs where city growth had exploded.

Again, as the pastor's wife, I struggled with negative, divisive people. I felt I had failed and let sadness cascade over me when things were said against my husband. I thought I had it conquered, but then it stuck its ugly head up again.

Lee was a good man, husband, father, and leader. I should know, I lived with him, and he walked the talk. He loved God, his family, the ministry, and me. He worked hard to build unity and have a healthy church to reach the community. In my attempt to keep our home a peaceful place for him, I kept a lot of things inside that should have been discussed. Didn't I learn my lesson several years ago? Some of the issues concerned my feelings of hurt, pain, disappointment, rejection, exclusion, frustration, setbacks, and more. As a result, these feelings were never brought to light.

I've never been sorry that I dealt with my issues like this, although at some time this will come out again. I learned how to **replace**. If I could replace all of the above issues with something good, I could keep the peace. An example of one issue was attending services. For me, facing the disgruntled people at church felt impossible. Therefore, I made up my mind to replace my feelings toward them. My four semesters of psychology in college helped in my understanding people, along with working in our Family Life Center in South Bend.

I treated them as if I felt sorry for them. After all, they had deep-seated problems to treat their leadership in such ways. I would smile, shake their hand, give them a hug, and might even give a "God Bless."

At first, I felt hypocritical, but then I dropped judging their deep-seated problems and put into practice principles of the Word. It felt right. The more we practice doing right, the more natural and real it seems, plus the results are gratifying.

Thank you, God, for instructions in your Word. They work!

In Nehemiah, chapters 1-4, we find the blueprint on how to rebuild. If you struggle with trying to rebuild a marriage, a relationship, a life situation, a defeat, or church breakdowns, take Nehemiah apart verse by verse. As Nehemiah saw a wall lying in ruin, he discovered God there for the rebuild.

Nehemiah [NIV]

1. Recognize the broken wall. (1:3)
2. Express your sorrow over the brokenness. (1:4)
3. Pray over the broken situation. (1:4b)Become a servant, a cup bearer. (1:11)
4. Is your heart sad?
5. Will sadness rebuild? Sadness is a choice. (2:2)
6. When fear comes—trust. (2:3)
7. Voice your request specifically. (2:5)
8. God provides safety. (2:7)
9. The enemy will come to discourage you and put doubt in your heart. (2:10)
10. Keep things to yourself. (2:16)
11. Work to rebuild. Be positive and confident. (2:18)
12. Keep pressing on. (2:19, 20)
13. Dedicate the wall to God. (3:1)
14. Keep on your guard at all times. (4:9)
15. Reorganize. (4:3)

16. Do not fear. God is great. (4:14b)

Dear God, thank You for life, relationships, and struggles we go through. This is where You can step in and put the broken back together, build that which has collapsed, make well the sick and hurting. When I think about this, my heart is full because You really love us enough to do this. I love the story of Nehemiah being obedient even when he couldn't see the end results. Give me faith to allow You to rebuild, reconstruct and repair what I cannot do. This is what You major in and I want the best that is You, Father-God. In Your Son's name, Amen.

Chapter 16
When the Cat's Away the Mice Play

(Aslan to the talking mice) "...You shall have your tail again."
~ C.S. Lewis in Prince Caspian

The church moved forward in spite of the opposition. Lee prepared to take a team to Africa and I chose to stay home. It wasn't necessary for me to go this time. A group of godly men planned to build a new structure for a newly-planted church. Those of us at home would be in prayer for that mission. However, you've heard the saying "When the cat's away the mice will play."

The disgruntled group at church in Dallas quickly held private meetings and tried to get a petition up for us to leave. Imagine how I felt. This group of about fifty didn't like us, didn't like our vision, and wanted us to leave. Alone with our daughter Tiffany, I tried to act like all was well. Now, it became humanly impossible to "replace" anything with this kind of betrayal.

The other staff wives and I continued meeting monthly for sharing and prayer for our different situations. These were wonderful women who loved God and ministry but were caught in a web of division. It just so happened we were having our monthly meeting at our home on the Monday morning after the Sunday when the division came to light. I didn't know how I could lead these women into encouragement and hope. After I dropped Tiffany off at school and got the house in order, stress swept over me. The ugliness spewed by those few people, crushed my lungs. I hyperventilated. I lay down on the floor thinking I might have to drive myself to the hospital. I had never hyperventilated in my life and I struggled to get my breath. I managed to crawl to the phone to call my mother and mother-in-law to pray for me. Within a few minutes, I felt a touch from the Master's hand. Slowly I relaxed. Maybe I could face the girls with hope.

While dressing, God's spirit spoke to my heart these words: *"Greater is He who is in you, than He who is in the world."* It is in times like this we need those reminders. I never saw the need to share this with the staff wives. It was my reaction, not theirs. The stress of conflict may leave us hollow, but there is nothing like the surging of God's power into our lives. My mother and Lee's mom were prayer warriors and I called upon them often.

The girls, as I called them, (Some of the staff wives were the age of my daughters.) gathered at our home. We sat around reading scripture, sharing, and praying for each other. We knew we were up against a force, BUT GOD fights for us!

I would recommend every pastor's wife organize a group of women, preferably staff wives, that can encourage, pray, and love each other. This time of bonding through scripture, prayer and encouraging words brought an empowerment. Our meeting time ended being lighthearted. Laughter is good medicine. Just out of the clear, a wild idea popped into my head. Some will criticize me for this but "For a time such as this"- it fit. I told the girls on the count of three to say an inappropriate word as loudly as they could so no one could understand it. Smiles came to their faces as they waited for the countdown.

"1, 2, 3," we all shouted our expletive at once. Words echoed. Laughter filled the room as we practically rolled on the floor in relief and release. Revived from this meeting of "the girls" I felt a renewed strength to overcome church politics.

I guess I had forgotten the words of Jesus: "love your enemies." Ouch! Whether unbelievers or backslidden believers, all need Jesus. I found we cannot change them, but we can control our reaction to them. The first time I prayed for someone who was a true divisive gem, I didn't want to do it. It was like taking a hard test and passing it- it felt right.

A group of men and their wives who literally took us under their wings during these trying times remain good friends. They held up our hands with love, encouragement, and outside interests. The leadership told Lee if we chose to leave, they understood. Everyone knew the division existed before we came. We wanted to leave this position, but God held us there for His purpose. Our District Leaders encouraged us, telling us they understood the political faction in the church and would continue to support us as we worked toward generating unity.

I know people in all walks of life have trials to walk through. It's not just those in ministry. At one point I said to Lee, "Why don't you go pump gas and I will hire out to clean houses? It would be better than this!" Our Goliath had multiplied.

How to Defeat the Enemy and Win Battles

I Samuel 17

1. David looked at Goliath (the problem) from God's perspective. (verse 45)

2. David remembered victories of the past. (verse 36)

3. Depend on God alone. (verses 39-40)

4. Proclaim the battle is the Lord's. (verse 47)
5. David obeyed and did what he knew he should do. (verses 48-49)

We loved Dallas, loved the warmth of the southern people. We connected with our staff, along with our faithful congregation who stuck it out in spite of the discord.

The time came for the congregation to vote on relocating the church to the northern suburbs or stay in our present location. When the vote was tabulated, eighty per cent voted to relocate to the northern suburbs. Over the next few months, the leadership chose to move the church to Carrollton. After the purchase of land and construction of the building, the new church opened its doors.

On the first Sunday, four hundred first-time visitors poured into the beautiful new church. Can you imagine the thrill of this passionate congregation who arrived that Sunday morning to a new beginning? This is why God brought us to Texas.

After a great victory, the body, soul, and spirit react to the challenge differently. Lee raced forward to make contact with those four-hundred first-time visitors and to fulfill God's Dallas plan.

I told you at the beginning of this book that women deal with things quite differently than men. Really? Yes, really! Exhausted in body, soul, and spirit from the "battle that was won," I collapsed—spiritually and physically. I never thought I would say the words, but I had lost joy. Empty, tired and no joy of the Lord—that loss weighed heavy on my heart.

Replace! I told myself. I tried to replace the empty weakness with many things, but it only worked for a short time. Then I slid back into a joyless state. Desperate for the joy of the Lord, I went back to my journals, searched where I had marked in my Bible, but nothing seemed to take hold.

Sometime later, we attended a missions' benefit in Colorado. Our daughter, Tami, and her husband John happened to be at the same benefit. The organization planned an event for the women during the first day. I just didn't want to go.

"Tami," I said, standing at the hotel door with my daughter. "You should go ahead."

"No, mom, I want to stay with you." Tami gave me a hug like only a daughter can give and then came into the room. "I feel like you're slipping back into discouragement. What's going on?"

The tears came. I sat down and told her. "I've lost the joy that only comes from the Lord."

"Well, Mom, what has given you joy in the past? What do you enjoy doing most in your life?"

Without thinking I said, "Striving to be a good wife and mother."

"Well, that's what you need to think on. Maybe share with young women God's way to be a good wife and mother." You could almost see Tami's mind working. "So many women need mentoring on this subject."

"That would be great, but what and how?"

She thought for a minute. "Give me two weeks and I will come up with a plan."

Within two weeks, Tami sent me a brochure made up of family home improvement tips." Her suggestion was to have the brochures available at church and set up times to coach women and families on family matters.

"Mom, you know the pastor of the church—I think his name is Reverend Lee Lebsack. You might ask him to make a one-time announcement about your new ministry."

She was right. I knew the pastor of our church well and thought he might work with me. Lee told the congregation, "God has spoken to Sharon's heart to offer a life coaching ministry."

Within a very short time, I began to feel the accomplishment of obeying God's call. This could benefit many of our church family who struggled with life's challenges. I felt God teaching me that life coaching was a vital need within the body of Christ. Not everyone needs counseling. However, mentoring or coaching seems to give most everyone a direction. God unfolded my purpose for this time of my life. The direction I had been searching for came to fruition. I've continued this coaching ministry even after retiring and still find it extremely gratifying.

How did I not realize it? God had been preparing me for this present time. True, I finally was fitting in and finding places to use my gifts, however, my healing in body, soul, and spirit continued. So many things fell into place. However, I could not find that total fulfillment. I did everything the Bible said to do. I read the Word, even though I didn't feel I connected. I literally stopped praying except at meal time. I told God, He knew my need and I would stop boring Him with my nagging request. I could fake it. After all, I had done that before, hadn't I? I kept busy, in fact, perhaps replacing this loss of joy with becoming addicted to adrenaline.

There were many happy moments that fooled me into thinking this was joy. Happiness and joy bring wonderful feelings to experience, but the two are very different. Joy comes when you know who you are. Happiness is based on other people, things, places, thoughts, and events.

I had myself convinced the "happy" would be enough. This wasn't right. Looking at others who had insurmountable challenges, I looked in the mirror and asked, *What in the world is your problem?* Although my purpose in life coaching helped tremendously, I wanted the full joy that I knew was possible with God. After all, Nehemiah 8:10 talks about "the joy of the Lord is our strength,"

The new church progressed with souls being saved every week. The Bible tells us how good and pleasant it is when God's people live in harmony. One day, Lee and I realized how many of our new attendees were sent by God to help with this growing church. Within a couple of years, our attendance had doubled, then tripled. We gave God all the glory and praised Him.

One Friday morning, I happened to be at home trying to read and study my Bible. There are times when the Word of God comes alive as you read a certain segment. I still searched for the fullness of joy, wanting the emptiness to be filled. I was talking to God about this very thing when the doorbell chimed. I looked out the peephole and saw my next door neighbor. We had tried to make contact with this family to no avail. Now, here the lady stood, wearing a cloak of despair.

I opened the door and she handed me a piece of mail that had fallen out of our mailbox. After seeing Lee's name on the front of the letter, she asked, "Is your husband a Reverend. Do you do counseling?

"I'm a Life Coach," I replied. Her next remark grabbed my attention.

"I prayed this morning if there was a God in Heaven, would He lead me to someone today to show me the way." Then very boldly she asked, "Do you pray for demonic powers to leave?"

I felt in my spirit this was truly an encounter with God. *Okay, Jesus, this is something new for the neighborhood. What's happening?*

I invited my neighbor into our home, but first she needed to run home to lock her door and would be right back. I called Lee, "PRAY! I'm having a prayer time with our neighbor."

"What, who, when, and why?"

"I can't talk now, JUST PRAY!"

I waited at the door until Judith came back. We walked into our family room.

Excited? Who would be excited at a time like this? ME! God was bringing people who needed Christ to my doorstep. We sat down and chatted for a few minutes, getting to know each other. She then proceeded to tell me about her childhood. She had attended a church service where she accepted Jesus into her heart and felt a joy that she had never experienced before. Her family forbade her from ever going back to that church.

"For thirty years, I've ignored God," Judith explained. "Now, I can no longer ignore him. I'm desperate. I prayed for the first time this morning and knew if there was a God, I needed Him now!"

Judith reaffirmed Jesus Christ as her personal Savior that morning, asking Him to release her of the demonic powers she felt. She asked me if I would be available to pray with her every Friday morning on her day off.

Judith grew in the Lord and started witnessing to her

husband and three teenage children. As a result of Judith's faith and faithfulness, her husband and children had an encounter with God.

Along with Judith's growth, the joy of the Lord flooded back into my life as never before. All I had to do was become a vessel to be used by my Lord and Savior. God had to get me to a place where I would be willing to literally get outside of myself and let God be God. Judith and I are friends to this day.

Years pass quickly when you're doing what you love. Why do I allow the weeds of life to overtake the beauty of life? Our daughters and sons-in-law had become strong believers, raising our grandchildren to love God with all their hearts.

These little ones are all perfect. However, I made the statement before, "There are no perfect people." But now, I will have to begrudgingly renege on that. Maybe there are perfect people called grandchildren.

Lee and I served this church for seventeen years, surrounded by great leadership—willing to persevere. This was a valley experience, but as soon as we started climbing the hill toward the mountain top—strength, hope, and vision became operative. There was a pause of calmness in our lives, and then Lee came home one day and made a bold statement, "Sharon, I'm going to the church board on Sunday to retire."

"Why?" I asked, remembering that he had recently thought of maybe pastoring two or three more years.

He went on to say, "With God's help, I feel we have accomplished bringing this church to a new level in growth and unity. It's time for someone else to take the church to the next level."

I blinked, shut my mouth and said, "Oh, okay! That's fine

with me."

Lee gave his resignation to the church, and it went smoothly. We were acquainted with a community close to the DFW area called Granbury, Texas. We made a couple of trips to visit that area and decided and found it to be a place where we could enjoy retirement. It filled the desire of my heart. All of our family lived close.

We put our home on the market and it sold within a few weeks. Lee's mom made the decision to move into a senior apartment complex in the DFW area as she didn't want to leave her church, friends, and community.

Things happened so fast my head switched to "frantic mode." We packed, purged things we had carried around for years, then found a home in Granbury.

One evening after an exhausting time of selling, buying, packing and leaving, I went out into our neighborhood and walked the streets. I had to let it out. It wasn't that I was sad, just emotionally and physically drained. Tired and exhausted, I sobbed to my Father. He comforted me, His Presence brought peace and mercy to my soul and I settled down.

One of the businessmen in our church owned a moving company and moved us to our new abode. At last, a move where no one interviewed us, checked us out, or expected anything from us. We even got to choose our own house. Imagine that! Would we love it or leave it?

At a going-away reception, many in the church family came to us, thanking us for sticking with them through one of the toughest struggles for a church to go through. Two men and women who stuck through the good and bad touched our hearts in a great way. I've never been one who lives on the accolades of others but we felt loved, respected, and accepted. This warm love still touches our hearts to this day.

Lee would still travel back for services on Sunday for the remainder of the month. Then everything stopped. Would retirement be all we expected? I need to pray—pray the way Jesus did. I love the King James version of the Lord's Prayer. However, The Message brings it into my need for today's problems.

Our Father which art in heaven, Hallowed be thy name.

Thy kingdom come, Thy will be done in earth, as it is in heaven.

Give us this day our daily bread.

And forgive us our debts, as we forgive our debtors.

And lead us not into temptation, but deliver us from evil:

For thine is the kingdom, and the power, and the glory, forever. Amen.

Matthew 6: 9-13 [KJV]

Our Father in heaven,
Reveal who you are.
Set the world right;
Do what's best—
As above, so below.
Keep us alive with three square meals.
Keep us forgiven with you and forgiving others.
Keep us safe from ourselves and the Devil.
You're in charge!

You can do anything you want!
You're ablaze in beauty!
Yes. Yes. Yes.
Matthew 6: 9-13 [MSG]

Part Five
Retirement

I thought growing old would take longer.

Sharon Lebsack

Chapter 17

No Longer a Pastor's Wife, But Still God's Child

"You are never too old to dream another dream! ~C.S. Lewis

Our journey took a sharp turn. Lee was no longer a pastor. Consequently, I was no longer a pastor's wife. The journey thus far had been God molding and making me into His plan for my life. He led me, held me, carried me, disciplined me, taught me, and loved me all the way. Some would say the roads traveled had many roadblocks—a lot of negative stories, but I want to be transparent. I want readers to understand the life of living with a public figure and learn from some of my experiences.

The first two weeks in our new home in Granbury seemed like a vacation. We leisurely unpacked, settled in, and even took time to go for a walk and for a golf cart ride. Lee and I both play golf and planned to enjoy living near a golf course. Lake Granbury isn't far from our home, and so we enjoy boating often. Hidden from the rest of the world, this little community is exactly what we needed.

Our adjustment from being extremely active to sedate activity was huge for me. Lee settled into retirement like he did everything—all the way. I didn't tell anyone I had been a pastor's wife until I had known them for some time. I wanted them to get to know me as just Sharon. After years of working with hundreds of people, you would think a quiet, unobtrusive lifestyle would bring contentment. The relief of not being accountable for a schedule, finding volunteers, activities, people, and places was a comfort. The freedom from that bit of bondage felt good. I was now a "former pastor's wife." This season of my life, however, would prove to be the most bittersweet of all.

Soon after getting settled in, I started to have a lot of extra time on my hands. I've said before that I was addicted to adrenaline—thus I had to have things to do. I washed all of the windows of the house every week. I did a spring cleaning every week. I washed my car every week. I found many things around the house like blankets, throws, and much more to launder. I searched for stains on clothing so that I might spend time getting them out.

Lee thought I had bought him a new vest one time. The brown vest had several spots on it, so what did I have to lose? The spots came out and Lee now had a beige vest. He loved it. However, he did think I was out of my mind. He had no way of knowing how obsessed with an activity I had become through the years. This was my escape routine. He would make statements like, "Sharon, you were never like this before!"

"Yes I was—you just didn't see it. Remember, you worked from daybreak to sundown and I did too, so we really didn't get the whole picture of one another's routine. That was church world--this world is known as Retirement 24/7. In case you hadn't noticed, I now have no one who needs me, no children, no mother-in-law."

After our children left for college and marriage, Lee's mother came to live with us until we retired. Upon moving to Granbury, she chose to stay in the DFW area and moved into a Senior Adult Living facility. If you are adding up those years– forty-two years, plus the five years we lived with other people–it was 47 years before our nest emptied. Let me help you get a clearer picture. We have two retirees/empty nesters trying to get to know each other in our 24/7 retirement season. Add to this the fact that I was now released from trying to be the perfect wife. Now I was free to voice my opinion openly. Poor Lee! That caused some getting acclimated to in this new season of our life together.

Finally, Lee said, "Sharon, we're going to have to live with each other the rest of our lives, so we must come up with a solution that leads to peace."

Together 24/7 could get monotonous, mundane, and even stuffy. There is always a solution for issues if you really want one. We first started having devotions and prayer every morning after breakfast together. Now that was another adjustment. We had each always fixed our own breakfast and were on our own for lunch.

An unstated plan formed in my head. Everyone would still be on their own for breakfast and lunch. I would keep the tradition of fixing a prime, nutritional meal for dinner. I love finding new recipes. Lee often teased me by asking, "Are we having a 'Food Network' meal tonight?" He chose not to partake of leftovers. Therefore, I had my lunch already prepared. I enjoyed having breakfast out on the patio, but he didn't. I decided we had a laborious road ahead.

One bright idea popped into my head as I was meditating on a plan to better understand our present state of affairs. We could pick an interesting book, with each of us reading a chapter at a time and then discussing that chapter together. This sounded like a great strategy for our dilemma. While I had Lee's full attention, I proceeded with another proposal of a rendezvous at The Coffee Shop. The proposed plan was accepted by my housemate and we soon started a book—*The Shack*. Our designated meeting place and time were scheduled on our calendar with both parties in agreement.

When coaching couples in the past, I would always recommend a marriage staff meeting at least once a week. Anything that required both parties' undivided attention would be saved for this meeting. Most couples discuss things "on the run" or with TV, children, cell phones, and much more going on in the background. Most likely nothing is resolved with all of the interruptions. Voices get loud, harsh words are spoken, and often anger interrupts the real reason for the discussion. Lee and I had used this marriage staff meeting method at different times. It's hard, but oh, so worth it!

I proposed that we also take this opportunity to discuss needs, issues, finances, family developments, and get our calendars in sync at The Coffee Shop. He agreed. We would often say, "Save it for The Coffee Shop." The plan worked and we enjoyed it so much that we started going to The Coffee Shop more than once a week. We were developing a different relationship than we ever had before, we experienced uninterrupted communication.

People were always coming and going in The Coffee Shop when others might be working on their computers or even conducting scheduled meetings. If anyone raised their voice everyone turned their head to check it out. If any anger was displayed, it was thought to be inappropriate. The Coffee Shop proved to be a perfect place for a marriage staff meeting.

It didn't take long until we recognized people that came for coffee at the same that we did. Lee gave private nicknames to many of them. We started smiling and speaking to those who seemed friendly. This was proving to be a two-fold rendezvous for marriage staff meeting and meeting people.

We had discussed earlier that we were not interested in making new friends. After all, we had our family which lived about one-and-a-half hours from Granbury. That was all we needed. It didn't take us long to come to the conclusion that we missed the closeness of our staff and close friends in Carrollton. The Coffee Shop provided the exact amount of involvement.

Church attendance brought the greatest change. Our goal was to attend a community-minded church with good preaching, worship, and a place to pay our tithes. It took a while, but we soon found a church that felt like home to us. We love it to this day. Lee and I have always been open and enjoyed getting acquainted with people outside our church. This broadened our aspect of getting into a rut. Soon, we bumped into some of our new acquaintances from The Coffee Shop at church.

I read somewhere in the Bible about Jesus having a diverse friendship base. Sometimes he ran with fishermen, doctors, prostitutes, liars, or crooked tax collectors. Everyone has a story and we both love this type of relational evangelism. We really love people, especially those that you can be yourself around.

Some of the people we met at The Coffee Shop were amazing—pilots, CEOs of companies, college professors, retired military, a few millionaires, artists, teachers, writers, and former NFL players with Super Bowl rings are just a few of the most interesting people we have ever met in our lives. We love hearing their stories and sharing our stories, too. We soon realized we needed people badly. It brought joy, happiness, and excitement to our life.

Living outside of the DFW area has great benefits and a few negatives. For one thing, the allergy level in Granbury was on a very high alert most of the time and Lee had to finally say, "Okay, I admit it, I'm allergic to trees."

The new doctor in Granbury had given Lee strong allergy medicines, along with steroid shots on two different occasions, back to back. He had a severe reaction, so I put him in the car and started driving into the DFW area to the hospital. We had a hospital in our little town, only fifteen minutes from our home, but I would be more comfortable at the DFW hospitals since we had lived in the area for seventeen years.

I made a bed for Lee in back of our car, had a small trash can beside him just in case. About ten o'clock at night, as I drove into the DFW Metroplex, he became nauseated and missed the can. "Didn't you see the can right beside you?" I had gone too far to turn back now. The journey was totally quiet until we approached the suburbs of Dallas when Lee started shaking violently and then fell on the floor of the car. Then he grew totally still and silent, not responding to my questions.

Speeding at ninety miles per hour, I blew my horn when going through stop lights, hoping a policeman would pull me over and escort us to the hospital. I just knew he'd had a heart attack and died. I used my cell phone to try to call our children but my mind wouldn't work trying to click on their numbers while speeding at 90 MPH. I finally reached our oldest daughter, Tami.

Frantically, I called out, "Your dad had a heart attack and died!" I explained, driving as fast as I could. My heart raced.

Tami handed the phone to John, our son-in-law, who calmly told me to stop the car, find a street address, and he would call 911. I did exactly what he said, and within five minutes an ambulance was right beside us. I told them my husband was on the floor. I was in shock. This was a living nightmare.

I got out of the car and one of the paramedics came to ask me about what happened. The other paramedic looked in the back seat and said, "He's alive!" I felt such a relief, tightness and fear drained from my mind and body. My daughter and son-in-law were still on the phone. I was so glad to tell them that Lee was alive. Grateful to God for sparing his life, I prayed that God would keep him alive.

A Las Colinas hospital was only one mile from that location. I followed the ambulance and found Lee lucid, with good reactions. The overdose of those medications almost caused his death. He was semi-conscious for four days in ICU, not remembering anything. Our family stayed with us all the time. What would we do without them?

On returning to "paradise" as we called our new community, the tranquility, beautiful pecan trees, and soothing lake brought healing from this enormous ordeal. Our spirits were high as we felt God had saved Lee's life. Our retirement season brought a new thankfulness, even though things weren't perfect. Recognizing small things like stars, moons, sunsets, grass, and budding flowers—life took on so much more meaning. We had really "stopped to smell the roses."

Can life get so fast and be cluttered to the extent that we miss the little things? Maybe that is what retirement is all about. We've stopped, we've looked, and we've settled.

A man who attended Tami and John's church in Wooster, Ohio wrote the following song, which I've hung onto for years and am just touched again by the beautiful reminder.

LITTLE THINGS THAT CHANGE A HEART

Sometimes it takes a small child before he can see
How much God sacrificed on the cross of Calvary.
God does "big things", yes they play a part.
God knows it's the little things that change a heart.

The Livingroom, the baby's cry,
A little tear in a grown man's eye.
Soon they've grown and off to school,
Running out the door "Mommy, I love you."
God knows it's the little things that change a heart.

Have we been too busy chasing after big things?
And forgotten the joy the little things bring?
God has to soften your heart to get a hold on you,
He doesn't use big things, small things will do.

The Bible says life is but a vapor, you know that's a fact,
Once the day is gone, you can't get it back.
So take time out, you might be surprised at the gifts that God gives,
If we will just open our eyes to the little things that can change a heart.

Dave Allyson©

Lee and I have come to a place where it is the little things that bring us closer to God. Someone has said, "Pressure is a good thing. It brings us to our knees."

We may have had something different in mind for our retirement years, but life is here and life is good. Perhaps God is asking us, "Did you really believe all of those sermons you preached? Did you really bring words of encouragement just to get a good feeling or because you really believed it?" Being tested is something we've learned down through the years. After a lesson has been taught, we take the test. We will find out quickly those who learned, those who cheated, those who just guessed, or the ones who truly applied the knowledge. They will have passed the test.

I so clearly remember my mother. Mama Kate (as her family called her) was in her late nineties when she fell and had to go into a nursing home. My mom had read the Bible through sixty-four times since finding Jesus as her personal Savior in her twenties. When talking with her, you would have thought she had graduated from a school of theology. In my eyes, she was a Saint. I could never measure up to her beauty in Christ. Her grandson Rusty and his wife Libby served as her caregivers during her last years, but her health became an issue and she required more help. As the decision was made on which facility would be best, we moved her into the new facility and prayed that she would be cared for and loved, daily.

"Sharon, I know why I have to go into a nursing home," Mama Kate said. "It's because I need more humbling before I go to meet my Maker."

"Mom," I replied, "you are already a very humble person."

"No, Sharon." She shook her head and then slowly said, "I'm a very prideful person."

If she thought she was prideful, what in the world does that make me? Perhaps in our retirement years, there is a need for being more humble—learning to be ministered to is an entirely different lesson from God. It seemed our life was moving in that direction.

The following week, we received some disturbing news. Our investment that we had planned for retirement went "belly up!" Most pastors have no retirement package other than Social Security. We thought we had invested in a very safe asset years ago, only to find out it had been mismanaged. Now we had nothing from our investment, only money going out. As the wife of a pastor, security is always sketchy. We had savings, but that would definitely not take us through retirement.

I felt like my life had turned upside down. Had we been so foolish in our investing? Why would God allow this to happen to us after years of faithful service? I cried, sobbed. I was a hurt, angry, retired pastor's wife.

We still had The Coffee Shop and that's where we talked about our dilemma. Our friends there became a lifeline to reality. We made ourselves go each week so we could laugh, share, and get to know our friends more. *And we thought we didn't need new friends.*

In the Midst of the Battle

In Acts, chapters 27 & 28, the Apostle Paul is a prisoner in the ship, but while imprisoned he is, in reality, a free man in Christ. Look at how Paul handled defeat and still remained in ministry. This portion of scripture is a great plan when feeling defeated.

1. The Storm (27:14-18)
2. Keep courage in spite of circumstances. (27:22)

3. Do not fear. (27:24)

4. Keep the faith. (27:25)

5. Be obedient to listen to God's instructions. (27:31)

6. Do not become weak from not eating. (27:33)

7. Give thanks always. (27:35)

8. Seek encouragement. (27:36)

9. There no doubt will be change in a storm. Be prepared. (27:39)

10. New plans may be needed. (27:40)

11. Attacks and setbacks will come. (27:41-42)

12. We all need hope. Ask God for it. (28:1-2)

13. Don't get too comfortable—attacks may continue to come. (28:3-4)

14. Shake off discouragement. (28:5)

15. Minister and glorify God in the midst of the storm. (28:7-8)

16. Your needs will be met. (28:10)

17. Your dream and vision may not always go like you want it to. Don't take that as a defeat. (28:11-16)

If we ever doubted that God would not take care of us, let me tell you a story of His divine interaction. Before retirement and moving to Granbury, our daughter Tonya (Lee's secretary) called me from the church office.

"Mom, does your bedroom suite need to be updated?"

"No," I responded. "Why?"

She went on, "Yes, it does! None of your furniture pieces match, do they?"

"Well, no, but it's fine."

"But, mom, this faithful family in our church called to inform us they have a bedroom suite at Haverty's Furniture that's waiting for you."

"What? Tonya, what do you mean?"

"Mom, this is something you need to do, the couple is meeting you at Haverty's in one hour!"

Lee and I got into our car and quickly drove to meet this couple, messengers of God reminding us how much He loves us.

Upon our arrival at the furniture store, we met the lovely lady who had called. We looked at the bedroom suite in awe—a king size, four-poster bed, along with a dresser and a mirror. With the set, stood another tall dresser, plus a large armoire. *This is a wonderful gift.* Nothing like this had ever happened to us.

"Do you need a dining room suite, Sharon?" the adorable lady asked.

"Not really, we've had ours about 40 years, but it is in good condition," I answered.

"You need a new updated one," she said. We went to another department and I asked if she would help me decide the style. Saying "thank you" didn't even touch the gratefulness within my heart.

I knew this was a God moment, but little did we know that God planned to double this blessing. Lee soon received a call from the same lady relating that she and her husband wanted to buy both of us a car for our retirement. Once again, during our entire ministry, we had never had anything like this happen to us. There is only one condition she made and that was for my car to be a convertible.

What? I had wanted a convertible my whole life but thought a pastor's wife would be ostracized for driving such a sporty car. At this time, we had no idea of what lay ahead in retirement. God always knows ahead of time our whole story. He knew the devastating situations which would be facing us after retirement.

Heavenly Father, It is a privilege to call You Father. You always take care of Your children, even when we don't know what's ahead. Thank You for looking ahead in my life, working to make the crooked roads straight. You always have the right people in my life at just the right time. I have thought maybe You have left me out there on my own, but You will never fail me nor forsake me. Let the words of my mouth and the meditations of my heart be acceptable unto You, Father. In Your Son's Name, Amen.

Sharon Lebsack

Chapter 18

Being Ministered To

"Not everything is meant for you to handle, trust God."
~ Charlie Brown

While trying to stay optimistic, we knew God had our back. We now had some lovely new furniture, two cars (paid for), and fortunately had enough to buy our retirement home (debt free). Lee and I both thought this couple, sent from God, had a premonition of what lay ahead for their pastor and his wife in retirement. Of course, they didn't, but God...!

We made adjustments and progress, and with the Coffee Shop meetings, some of our unpleasant situations settled down. God had been there every step of the way. Perhaps now was a good time to search for a neighborhood Bible study and "girlfriend fellowship." One of my neighbors, Sandy, had been having a Bible study in her home for a couple of years. I asked if there was room for one more.

"Of course, we would love to have you join us every week," she said.

I admit, I felt slightly awkward not being in charge. God has a sense of humor saying, "Well, Sharon, you've got your wish, no more pastor's wife duties. This group of women accepted me as just one of the neighbors. I eventually told them I was a former pastor's wife. Now they thought I knew every answer to every question about spirituality, unanswered prayer, healing, salvation, and on and on. I soon had a phrase I used, "let's look that question up this week and all come back with what we've found."

Out of this group, one of the women shared about her ongoing illness. Many of her friends didn't know what to do with her medical problems, so they just left. My heart hurt for this little lady. I told her to choose a few women friends from our Bible study, invite them to her home, and we would have a Women Encouraging Women group (WEW). She was ecstatic. She called me the next day and said she had about ten women who were gung-ho to begin this support group.

Whether you have doubt and fear or have just lost heart, remember:

GOD HAS HIS HAND ON YOU, LIVE TODAY AS IF IT WAS YOUR LAST.

1. Love and be kind to those close to you.
2. Leave a Legacy.
3. Stay close to God and He will stay close to you.
4. Study the Word in order to learn His ways and promises.
5. Don't doubt God.
6. Give Him all praise, honor, and glory.
7. Be alert for those with whom you can share Christ.
8. Be an encourager.
9. Find your purpose and move in it.
10. Believe in God. Believe in Yourself!

This WEW group met regularly for five years. Lives were enlightened, encouraged, and educated. We would select topics or books—read, study, and apply them to our lives. This dear lady received acceptance of exactly where she was in life. My heart was happy as women were becoming knowledgeable when studying and applying God's Word. Others heard about the group and wanted to be a part. The WEW group found that encouraging others boomeranged right back at them. It felt good to apply the Bible in this aspect.

At the end of the five-year period, I felt God releasing me from the leadership. This experience was like a bridge crossing from pastor's wife to a Christian woman exercising my gifts. I felt in charge of my own life.

Right in the middle of this time-frame, Lee had gone into Dallas for a test from our cardiologist. It was supposed to be a simple test. I was sitting out in the waiting room when a nurse came to tell me I could come back to see my husband. When I got back to his space, he said, "I have to have triple bypass surgery." I thought he was kidding. I almost laughed, until I saw the anxious look on his face.

"Are you kidding me?"

"I'm not kidding," he responded seriously. Another unexpected event in our retirement. God went ahead of us. He didn't have a heart attack and this surgery would take care of the blockage. Thank you, Jesus!

Again, our family supported us in every way. Lee and I thank God every day for each of them being there with love, prayer, much concern, and care. How blessed can we be? They are ministering to us instead of us ministering to them.

After almost a week of Lee's hospital stay, coming back to

paradise was not quite as exciting as when we first came. One of my dear friends had been talking about a daily devotional book that spoke to her heart while going through a challenging ordeal. The devotional was called *Jesus Calling* by Sarah Young. We picked up the book and read it every morning for devotions during Lee's rehabilitation. While reading the daily devotional, we would look at each other and say, "How can this be, that's exactly what we needed today." It's not what we had planned, but we had been prepared for this season of our life.

One of our neighbors, Fluffy Anderson, lost her husband unexpectedly. The loss was devastating. Lee and I took her a *Jesus Calling* devotional book. This visit opened up a special beginning for a delightful relationship with our Christian neighbor. One day Fluffy shared with me that she had given out over sixty copies of *Jesus Calling* to those in need. What a witness! Fluffy started bringing us a loaf of homemade banana nut bread every other week. Do we look forward to this gift of love? You betcha! What a thrill to watch Fluffy walk through the death of her husband step-by-step, releasing her life, circumstances, and struggles to God.

I love a particular conversation between Peppermint Patty and Charlie Brown from the *Peanuts* comic strip.

Peppermint Patty says, "Sometimes, I feel like I've done all I can."

Charlie Brown answered, "Then it might be better to walk away and let God do it. Not everything is meant for you to handle. Trust God."

Our children need to see how we choose to go through earthly disappointments. Life is life. We're not promised a rose garden, we are only promised His presence, His care, His comfort, and His counsel. Until you get to this season of your life you can't imagine the apprehension that you face in body, soul, and spirit. Retirement is meant to be "resplendent," and much of it does not disappoint you, but let's look at some of the things that we face:

- Grey hair exposing itself. "Oops! Now it's falling out."
- You may lose strength and balance.
- Teeth get older too—fillings, bridges, partials may be needed.
- All print is now smaller. "Where did I leave my readers?"
- "I can't hear you!"
- "Why do they have it so cold in here? Every place I go I have to take a jacket."
- "I don't remember you telling me to pick up the dog."
- "This new cream guarantees it erases wrinkles—not!"
- "Why is my body starting to look like this? I hardly recognize myself!"
- "Why is it that these 'old people' are so negative and only want to talk about their issues?"

Because of facing these changes in our life, we could become negative. We don't want to become negative. And we don't have to be negative. **Replace!** It works. If we practice the rule of "Replace," we have a choice of looking on the other side of the problems mentioned in the paragraph above.

1. **The silver-hair is a crown of glory. Proverbs 16:31a [NIV]**
2. **With the ancient is wisdom; and in length of days**

understanding. Job 12:12 [KJV]

3. They still bear fruit in old age; they shall be fat and flourishing. Psalm 92:14 [KJV]

4. So we do not lose heart. Though our outer self is wasting away, our inner self is being renewed day by day. 2 Corinthians 4:15 [NIV]

5. Do not cast me off in the time of old age; forsake me not when my strength faileth. Psalm 71:9 [KJV]

6. The aged woman likewise, that they be in behavior as becometh holiness... that they may teach the young women to be sober, to love their husbands, to love their children. Titus 2:3-4 [KJV]

As retirement slowed down, days were long, life was short. I got mired down in the small things of life. I couldn't relax and constantly did unnecessary busy-work. I thought for me to be fulfilled, my days needed to be filled to the brim.

The next few years brought us two more grandchildren, Jackson and Avery. Oh, don't tell me it's true—four great-grandchildren: Brynley, Haven Grace, Lyla, and Cole joined our family. I love the joy that these precious children bring to my life. "If I had a star for every reason I love my grandchildren, I would own the entire night sky!"

In looking back on every situation we have gone through in retirement, we saw God hold us above the stormy waters. It's astonishing how God spoke to Lee's heart one day to retire the next week. Life would have been overwhelming if we had to go through the health issues while still pastoring. God always looks after His own.

I've often heard people quote a phrase "God will not put on

us more than we can handle." In researching this I found it nowhere in the Bible. But what I did find was the verse some have taken out of context.

All you need to remember is that God will never let you down; he'll never let you be pushed past your limit; he'll always be there to help you come through it. I Corinthians 10:13 [MSG]

Father God, I come before You humbly because of who You are and not who I am. It is not about me, but sometimes it really seems like it, doesn't it? Forgive me for the times I've asked You why You planned the last part of our lives like You did. Please, forgive me again, because sometimes I keep wondering. It is becoming more clear the closer I get to You. My trust is in You because You created, cared and carried me from the beginning. As I look back I see that and as I look forward I believe that. Thank You and may You be glorified. Amen.

Sharon Lebsack

Chapter 19

Paradise Found

Retirement: When you quit working, not living.
~ Unknown Author

As life settled down again in "Paradise," we were excited about our replacement plan. Lee had recovered remarkably from open heart surgery. Now, in total retirement mode, he worked out at the fitness center, played golf a couple times a week, and ran errands (one time to get the bolt and the next time to get the nut). The Coffee Shop remains one of his favorite adventures of the day. He loves it when Jim, Moon, Kevin, and Walt are there to solve all the problems of the world.

Here is a list of recommendations for good health that I have used down through the retirement years:

1. Get a medical checkup.
2. Eat balanced, nutritional foods.
3. Get enough sleep.
4. Work out: walk, swim, lift weights, and join a gym or the YMCA.
5. Listen to uplifting music.

6. Take in God's creation.

7. Read the Bible, pray, meditate, and find a good devotional book.

8. Join a support group.

9. Reach out to someone in need: a visit, a phone call, an email, deliver a meal, send a card. You will receive more than you give out.

10. Make sure you have a hobby: sewing, knitting, crocheting, painting, gardening, cooking, baking, canning, quilting, photography, create jewelry, golfing, tennis, and much more. Just find something to enjoy that brings fulfillment.

11. Go on day trips to various close towns and/or an extended trip.

12. Email and Facebook friends and relatives, stay relevant.

13. Read books. Join a book club.

14. Volunteer in church, hospitals, schools, other community projects.

15. Go to plays, operas, community entertainment, and events.

16. Play card or board games. Take dance, singing, guitar lessons, or others that you may have an interest in.

17. Go shopping (just to look or buy).

18. Teach a class (unlimited).

19. Visit grandchildren, attend their activities, bring them handmade gifts, and send them letters.

20. Write a book.

My replacement work for full-time ministry had to be intense, I could tell. I've always thought I was quite comfortable with change, but this is huge. I soon called my high school friend, Jo, who lives in Florida, to have her bring back to my memory how to cast on stitches for knitting. I had not knitted since high school, but I could do this with YouTube and Jo. I made scarves, hats, shawls, fingerless gloves, glass holders, purses, and baby blankets, appliqued objects on shirts for grandchildren, plus made dresses and hats for grandkids and great-grandkids. I made wooden crosses, covered them with a colored cement. Then I placed strategically broken pieces of jewelry on them and called them "Broken Pieces."

Over the next few years, a couple of shops on the Granbury Square carried my goods until I ran out of products and couldn't keep up with making my handcrafted items. I decided just making things for my family would do. I'm sure there were plenty of my handcrafted items that were not exactly what they would have picked out, wanted or even liked, but they were always lovingly accepted. It kept me creating and fulfilled.

I actually settled a bit in my new season of life, although something was missing. I've realized that nothing is going to bring total fulfillment for me on this earth because it is not my final resting place. That little void is almost always there, even when I use my "replace" technique. Since I do not enjoy TV, I searched to fill that time when most people settle down after dinner for relaxation. I relax by doing projects. Then about 8:00 or 9:00 in the evening, I sat in the family room to watch a couple of TV programs and news before bedtime, which I resisted. Don't get me wrong, I love being rested with energy, I just don't like to stop doing things. I know I'm weird. The addiction I have allowed to rule my life at times has been adrenaline. If you are a psychologist reading *The Confessions of a*

Pastor's Wife, let's meet up sometime for a consultation.

As you remember, the first part of this book alluded to much travel. I guess we did enough travel for a lifetime, therefore we do very little traveling in retirement.

My friend Elizabeth and I have met up at The Coffee Shop for several years. At different times she would mention a Bible study group of women from our church, assuming I would enjoy the group. She was not a bit pushy, no doubt just realizing I needed something like that. I found the name of the group quite amusing—the Turtle Sisters. Well, I no doubt would be embarrassed to tell anyone I attended a Bible study called "The Turtle Sisters."

I distinctly remember the day I brought up the subject with a question, "When does this group meet?" I couldn't say Turtle Sisters yet. She told me more about the group and I made a decision to go with her to the next meeting.

The first time I attended I thought I wouldn't return. Everyone was very friendly and accepting of me as Elizabeth's friend, Sharon. I went again a second and third time, reluctantly. I finally committed to attend and discovered exactly where the Turtle Sisters got their name. It made sense now, but it's still hard to call yourself a turtle. Their name came from the Roman armor and the shell of a turtle. There are several places in the Bible which speak about the Armor of God. One is found in Ephesians.

Above all, taking the shield of faith, wherewith ye shall be able to quench all the fiery darts of the wicked. Ephesians 6:16 [KJV]

The Roman soldiers would hold their shields, made of wood and leather, in front of them as a protection from spears or javelins, arrows, swords, or daggers. But when the enemy launched flaming missiles, they dipped the shield in water, placed hooks on the sides and connected with those next to them. This would form a damp, dense shell of protection called the turtle formation. The technology of armor has changed today, but the principle remains the same—protect the wearer during battle.

The Apostle Paul speaks of the Roman armor as a protection. The Bible tells us we are in a war fighting to protect ourselves from Satan, the devil, who seeks ways to destroy Christians. Paul warns us to beware of Satan's devices. He advises us to put on the whole armor of God. Paul draws a strong comparison between a Roman soldier's armor and the spiritual armor of God.

Here come the turtles lined up for battle with their shells (shields) protecting them from predators. These shields make it difficult for many predators, such as raccoons and others, to get a bite of tasty turtle meat. Many land turtles can draw their legs, tail, and head into their shells. Instantly recognizable by their protective shell, the turtle's shell is different from other animals. The turtle's shell is attached to its spine and lower rib cage as a permanent suit of armor.

The Turtle Sisters put on their full armor of God and help each other when discouragement, life's challenges, and family situations come their way. They have a picture of joining together by placing their shields next to each other as they pray, encourage, read God's word, and love. They pray for protection from predators.

Two years into Turtle Sisterhood I embrace the name. We meet once a week for Bible study, have home prayer groups, call on each other when a need arises, and go for coffee at The

Coffee Shop. We are there for whoever may need an encouraging word, prayer or just a hug. It is the most refreshing group of sisters. I forgot to mention most of these women are in their 50s and 60s. I'm the elder of the group. We have a lot of humor, which keeps us laughing. We cry. We hug and text often. Many times we're all praying at the same time at different places. Take today, for example, one of us is in the hospital having a cancerous lump removed. We all prayed at 9:00 this morning in unison, connecting our shields for our sister. Tomorrow, we're going on one of our day trips to Chip and Joanna Gaines' Magnolia Extravaganza in Waco, Texas. Everything is bigger in Texas!

Retirement, as with other seasons of my life, has proven to be a time of growth in my Christian walk. My days of developing are still in progress. God has been patient and kind but still, has a big job in front of Him with me. I'm excited and looking forward to more of God, His plan, and new beginnings.

Dear Father in Heaven:

Trusting in You changes everything, Lord. I need Your help in not dwelling in the past or fearing the future. Right now is my most important time frame. I want to learn to worship You better. Help me to seek Your ways more earnestly. Let my thoughts and my actions be pure in Your sight, Lord.

I see the day ahead and imagine ways to improve. I will look for people who need encouragement. I will surround myself with those who are uplifting and give encouragement from Your Word. I will watch for the opportunities and moments You offer to teach me more about You.

I know You love me Lord and know You are aware of my situation right now. In our retirement, we had no idea what would come our way, but you knew. Thank you for turning the undesirable circumstances, into something good, something beyond our comprehension. We felt as if we were drowning, but You renewed our strength as we swam toward You. Because of Your love for me I'm learning to trust You. Thank You, Father. In Jesus' Name, Amen.

Sharon Lebsack

Part Six
Other Pastors' Wives

The role of a pastor's wife is unique. Certainly, other pastors' wives have their own stories to tell. I asked several to share an experience in their own journeys.

Each of these women has influenced my life in some way. They were comrades who fought the good fight. We all encountered bumps in the road, roadblocks, detours, or an unexpected situation that completely altered our destination. My thanks to each of you who bravely showed your vulnerability in relating something of what goes on behind the scenes. You will offer encouragement and inspiration to those who are on a similar path. Thank you for sharing some of your experiences with me and my readers.

Sharon Lebsack

Chapter 20

Tami

By Tami Bullard

To everything there is a season, and a time to every purpose under the heaven. Ecclesiastes 3:1 [KJV]

I grew up in the church. My parents, and my dad's parents were both in the ministry. When I was 18, I married a man who was called into ministry. My life revolved around the church—my life became the church.

For three years, John and I served on staff at my dad's church in South Bend. This was to our benefit for furthering our experiences which would prepare us for pastoring our own church. When my parents moved to a new area of ministry, he advised us to find a church, as he felt we were ready to pastor. John and I served in three different churches in Michigan, Ohio, and Texas. Pastoring our own church proved to be much harder than being on staff. I went through times of defeat, dejection and some depression. God had placed a call upon my life for ministry and I wanted to work in my strengths and gifts wherever needed. I loved people and loved working as secretary, worship leader, women's director and more. I was highly motivated to be a helpmate to John and serve wherever I could.

Each church that we pastored had great growth in numbers and discipleship. Not to say without many mountains to climb, many valleys to plunge through, and pick-me-ups from falling into disappointments, dejection, and depression. I'm sorry to say, I expected too much from the Christian Community. After several years, I came to the realization that I could not and would not put high expectations on church members. We're all human, non-perfect people, Christian or not. In the job force, I've had some of the same disappointments as in church leadership.

At one point in our first pastorate, I came close to a breakdown. Remarks about my husband or our leadership threw me into self-pity, disappointment, and sorrow. Whenever you are a leader in any situation there are those who don't agree with your vision, power struggles for leadership, unhappiness in their lives causing them to lash out, and then there are just "mean people." If this isn't dealt with, it can bring you to a place of blaming God. I'm so thankful I never let it get to that point. I made a trip to visit my parents and felt time away under their mentoring and love would give me a different way of looking at our situation. My parents pointed out that this was not abnormal in a church setting.

Eventually, we decided that we wanted our children to have the opportunity to be near family and we were ready for a break in ministry. We moved to Texas where John got a job in the corporate world. We attended my dad's church. I began to heal emotionally with family love surrounding me. I began a new career. This decision worked for my good and I felt led in a new direction with a different purpose.

John returned to the ministry for 13 years serving in various supporting roles as business administrator, staff pastor, executive staff pastor and then became lead pastor. I again became a pastor's wife but without the associated responsibilities in the church. Good things had been happening, the church was growing. With these changing times, John had to address some serious issues with the staff concerning leadership, respect, and loyalty. A storm was brewing and the tides in the church were turning.

There was a choice to be made: stay and fight the battle which might split the church or step out of full-time ministry. My entire life had been defined by the church--for better or worse, richer or poorer, in sickness and health. The church had become more than a building, more than a congregation and more than a house of worship, it had been our home and family.

However, we felt that it was the time for a break in ministry. God had another plan for our lives. It was not an easy transition. We submerged ourselves in our children, grandchildren and turned to our family for comfort, healing, and support. John found work in the corporate world.

We are still called to be in ministry but in a different way. We have peace in our hearts and know God has opened new doors. This season of our lives is for providing prayer, support, and guidance to our family and others. We are able to minister with love and encouragement to those we come in contact with in our daily lives.

We will pick up the torch from my parents and leave a legacy of the love of God for our children. God is everything to me. I face the future not on what is seen, but on what is unseen since what is seen is temporary, but what is unseen is eternal.

Tami Bullard is the eldest daughter of the author of this book. She was a preacher's kid and married a full-time youth associate pastor. Tami assisted and supported her husband John in full-time ministry for thirty-two years. The Bullards have been married for thirty-five years, have two children and three grandchildren.

Currently, Tami and John both work corporate jobs, love spending time with their families, and have learned to relax and enjoy every moment life brings them.

Chapter 21

Joy

By Joy Headley

Let your conversation be always full of grace, seasoned with salt, so that you may know how to answer everyone.

Colossians 4:6 [NIV]

The "gift" of gab is my daily struggle. Learning what to say and when to say it has been a huge challenge.

During one of the first few months that my husband was the senior pastor at our church, I volunteered for some office work. I made an offhand comment about how I didn't like green paper for handouts. The next time I came into the office I saw a sign that said:

Do not run copies on green paper.

I went to one of the office assistants and asked why green paper can't be used.

"You are the senior pastor's wife," she said. "If you don't like green paper, we won't use it."

My face reddened with embarrassment. I had no idea that the staff would take my comment so seriously. Because I said I didn't like green paper, no green paper. I quickly let them know they were free to choose any color of paper.

Another time, I attended a baby shower in our fellowship hall. A larger crowd than anticipated attended, and we ran out of chips and dip—my favorite foods. Half joking, I commented, "I'm so disappointed! My favorite snacks are gone. I sure hope next time we plan better."

Within twenty-four hours, I had a number of calls explaining how difficult it was to plan a shower. I was told that if I was going to criticize and blame, they just wouldn't be having more showers or parties. Once again, the weight of my words had a serious impact. I had to learn to curb my words—to think before I spoke.

I learned the importance of knowing that, as a pastor's wife, my words should be an example of love and encouragement. I realized that when I spoke, it was the pastor's wife speaking and to some people that was a big rock. My words carried weight. I thought my words were like pebbles on the playground, but too many of our church family, what I said felt like a big rock. I prayed and asked God for help. Over the years, God helped me to be cautious with my tongue so that my words speak of God's love and grace.

When transition happens in our lives, we especially have to be aware of our words and the emotions attached to them. Recently, my husband was elected as a district official and we are in the process of saying goodbye to thirty-four years of ministry at our church in Dallas.

My emotions and my words are an integral part of planting seeds of hope, encouragement, and faith to our church family as they mourn the leaving of their pastors. God lead us to allow me to be the transition pastor during a season while the pulpit committee is formulating the next steps.

As transition-pastor, God wants me to be a hope dealer in every situation. I honestly shared how hard it is for me to come on campus, preach, and teach without my husband. But God's love, joy, and peace are so rich when we sacrifice our feelings and follow His calling and purpose—hope happens. My daily habits of devotional times alone with God, sharing my feelings with trustworthy friends, and by walking in faith I line up with God's will, not my feelings. Life can be a battle, but I am so thankful that we are overcomers because of the power of God.

Over the years, the Holy Spirit has been a great teacher, and my husband has taught me by example. Words are a powerful tool and can impact beyond comprehension, especially in the way they are perceived by others. I realized my words as the pastor's wife were so much more significant to others than I had ever imagined.

I have learned that what one says can be misinterpreted or misunderstood.

Joy Headley is a pastor's wife, educator, mother, and grandmother. She finds great pleasure in mentoring and coaching others so their life stories can be victorious.

Sharon Lebsack

Chapter 22

Judy

By Judy Hayburn

Rejoice always; pray without ceasing; in everything give thanks; for this is God's will for you in Christ Jesus. Faithful is He who calls you, and He also will bring it to pass.
1 Thessalonians 5:16-18, 24. [ESV]

Everyone in ministry needs an intercessor. My husband, Mark, and I served as missionaries in Africa for many years. During our first furlough in 1987, a prayer warrior came into our lives. In her eighties, Alta Stahn attended a small church in Huntington, Indiana. We visited her church for a missionary service where Mark preached, I testified, and we sang "Greater is He Who is in You." At the conclusion of the service, this sweet little old lady introduced herself and said that she was an intercessor for us and that she prayed for our family every day.

We kept in touch with Alta over the years, mostly through letters and a few phone calls. In 1994, a serious family situation developed regarding our daughter Jennifer. We desperately wanted to get in touch with Alta, to ask her to pray for us.

However we didn't have her phone number with us.

That night, Mark and I sat in our hotel room on the back side of the Arizona desert and cried out to God. We prayed, trying to figure out who we could call to get her number when the phone rang. This was particularly surprising because very few people knew where we were. Alta's voice rang out. She had been trying to find us. God had given her a message for us.

Overwhelmed with joy and thanksgiving that she had obeyed the Lord and found us to deliver this message, she continued, "Praise Him and He will intervene and do incredible things for your family." Her words flowed out with joy. "While I prayed for your family, the Lord told me to call Mark and Judy Hayburn and give them this message."

Mark and I burst into tears of joy and thanked her so much for calling us with this word from the Lord. We felt the peace of God fill our hearts and as we praised and worshipped the Lord with confidence knowing that God was in control of the situation. In fact, this was a huge turning point for our daughter. Jennifer has since faced life's disappointments and challenges with a courageous faith in God.

Even though I have never been a lead pastor's wife, I have been a missionary's wife. It is relatively similar. The missionary's wife is tested, interviewed, and expected to work alongside her husband in whatever field of missions they are sent. We are separated from our family in the states (children, parents, grandparents) for four years. All of your belongings are put into a container to last you those four years. After that period of time, you come back to the states for one year to raise money by speaking at different churches. This money takes care of our housing, car, medical, and other expenses over this period of time. God called Mark and I both to missions and we have worked through the disappointments, relational adjustments, loneliness, illnesses (in another country), and cultural differences to the point of loving our years as missionaries to the continent of Africa.

We learned to never allow fear to enter our minds when disappointments came or we were faced with impossible situations. We have made it a practice to trust God, praise Him in everything, and always thank Him in advance for working things out for our good. We know that God truly does have our good in His plan. God always knows where we are and what we need.

Judy Hayburn has been a missionary with her husband, Mark, for over 30 years. She has developed a curriculum for Christian marriage and family. This course has been approved by Global University, USA, as a transfer of credit courses at the BA level and is used in Bible schools in Kenya, Malawi, Ethiopia, and South Africa. The title of the course is **God's Blueprint for Marriage**. *Judy is a recognized independent facilitator of* **Parenting the Love and Logic Way.**

Sharon Lebsack

Chapter 23

Darla

By Darla Yannatone

"For I know the plans I have for you," declares the Lord…
Jeremiah 29:11 (NIV)

Disillusionment, self-pity, and hopelessness swirled in my mind, mirroring the winter weather that whirled around me. Looking forward to just getting away, connecting with friends, and hopefully, a chance to clear my mind, I headed for a long weekend of work.

In the days before everyone owned a cell phone, while waiting for a layover in the Dallas airport, I searched for a pay phone. As I walked away from the pay phone, I saw a guy I had dated in high school. I hadn't seen him in more than twenty years. What were the odds of us being on the same plane, headed for the same destination city and seated beside each other? How does that happen?

The hour-long flight in the dimly lit plane gave us a chance to catch up and share our life's stories and the feelings that accompanied them. He, too, was disillusioned with marriage and life. The security and commonality we felt with each other were a powerful attraction and a temptation to somehow rekindle a relationship.

I spent the weekend in Missouri striving to get the enormous workload done, tossing and turning with emotional turmoil as my pillow. On the flight home, I was an emotional basket case. Prior to boarding the plane that evening, I had slipped a piece of the day's mail in my purse.

On the first leg of my flight, I had read that card containing the verse *For I know the plans I have for you," declares the Lord, "plans to prosper you and not to harm you, plans to give you hope and a future."*

God's word helped me, but my own desire to suppress any problem pushed my feelings down. Determined not to tell my husband, Dave, about this unexpected event, guilt crushed in on me. Not for my actions. I did nothing, but I felt disappointed in my marriage and wanted to hide it. I returned home—distant, cold, and exhausted. It soon became apparent to Dave that something was preoccupying my mind, so he probed. My secret encounter poured out of me.

The subsequent days were some of the most difficult and painful we had ever experienced. Dave and I talked through the issues and events that brought us to this place.

Two very different people, an extroverted Italian city kid and an introverted Dutch farm girl, with a mutual love for

God and ministry, had met and married. God had blessed us with two beautiful and healthy daughters. We enjoyed wonderful opportunities and great friends. However, our differences made for many conflicts in our home. Since we suffered from an inability to resolve our conflicts, we simply had spent years burying them.

This time of crisis made it necessary for us to deal with the issues. One of the initial things we did was to seek godly, biblical counseling, both separately and as a couple. I felt safe to share with this counselor the feelings that I had buried for so long. Dave and I both began to learn that neither of us was right or wrong—we were just different. We learned to adjust our expectations.

However, the greatest personal takeaway from this two-year healing process became a fresh relationship with God. The words in **Jeremiah 29:11-14** became my personal lifeline. When feelings of despair would come to mind, I recited that Scripture, often many times a day. God's word is reliable and true. I learned the necessity of taking my fickle thoughts and sometimes deceptive feelings captive.

Now, years later, I give praise to God for rescuing us. We addressed and resolved persistent conflicts and learned ways to manage differences. I give Jesus my heart, and whatever it contains, on a daily basis—whether frustration, joy, strife, confusion, burdens, awe, or whatever is there. Acknowledging it and giving it to Him has become a part of my daily time with God.

For I know the plans I have for you," declares the Lord,

"plans to prosper you and not to harm you, plans to give you hope and a future. Then you will call on me and come and pray to me, and I will listen to you. You will seek me and find me when you seek me with all your heart. I will be found by you," declares the Lord, "and will bring you back from captivity.[a] I will gather you from all the nations and places where I have banished you," declares the Lord, "and will bring you back to the place from which I carried you into exile." Jeremiah 29:11-14 [NIV]

In June 2016, Darla Yannatone and husband David celebrated 45 years of marriage and ministry. The Yannatones served on the Lebsack's staff as youth pastors for several years. Darla worked alongside her husband in body, soul, and spirit. They have two daughters and five grandchildren. Dave currently serves as a staff pastor at First Assembly of God in Fort Myers, FL. Together Dave and Darla enjoy walking, playing games, and spending time with their family.

Chapter 24

Kate

By Kate Guajardo

I love food! I love eating food. I love shopping for food. I love cooking food. I love watching shows about food. So it was no surprise to me when the Lord used a food documentary I found on Netflix to speak to me about my life and my role in His Kingdom.

At this Netflix point in my life, I had been a pastor's wife for about six years. We married right out of Bible college and went straight into full-time youth and young adult ministry. Early on the Lord gave me a verse that I feel sustained me through the early tedious years of ministry.

Let us not become weary in doing good, for at the proper time we will reap a harvest if we do not give up. Galatians 6:9 [NIV]

It did not take long for the newness of being in the ministry to wear off and this verse quickly became my fuel. I would show up to service after service, week after week, meeting after meeting telling myself "I will reap a harvest, I will reap a harvest, I will reap a harvest!" I felt like the Little Engine That Could, chugging along through days and weeks and years, where all I could cling to was the promise that God had spoken clearly to me, "(There will be) a harvest if we do not give up!" Seasons of ministry flew by. Exciting and fun seasons, busy and exhausting seasons, dry and lonely seasons, painful and long seasons flowed through my life.

In that later season filled with painful and lonely moments, I found myself flipping through Netflix and stumbling onto an episode of *Mind of a Chef*. Little did I know I hadn't just stumbled onto a documentary about a wheat crisis in our agricultural system, but that I was about to have an encounter with the Holy Spirit.

Apparently, in our genetically modified modern culture, getting our hands on pure untouched wheat is extremely rare. The host of *Mind of a Chef* interviewed one of the few farmers who harvest this pure form of wheat. Glued to the television screen, I listened as he explained the process and showed each season of sowing the seed and reaping the harvest. He summed it all up with words that suddenly seemed to take my breath away. He looked at the host soberly and explained,

"Every season I must put the last of my pure seeds into the ground and hope that it produces another harvest."

Instantly, that one phrase spoke volumes to my soul as the Holy Spirit began to take my attention off the television and onto what God wanted me to hear.

Ministry is the job of a sower. We tirelessly work our fields, scatter seed, tend the crops, and then we pray and ask the Lord to bring the harvest.

I waited for a point in our journey that had been painful and long. We were weary! We had worked the fields. We had scattered seed. We had tended the crops. We had sought the Lord, but harvest wasn't coming. In fact, it seemed as though we lost more crops than we reaped. I had clung to the promise in Galatians so tightly, knowing that God would be faithful to His word. In the depths of my heart I knew it was true. However, I doubted it for my church. Maybe for us, in this season, at this church, with these people, maybe that formula for harvest just would never successfully produce.

The Holy Spirit used that one line from the wheat farmer to bring me a life-changing moment. The Lord tenderly asked me, "Are you willing to plant again?" Was I willing to take the last of what I felt like I had in me to give and offer to the Lord, put it in the ground, bury it, and trust that He would do something with it? It required an act of surrender. One like I had never experienced before. The Lord asked nothing tangible of me. I knew it was a surrender of my plans, my timeline, my pride, and my dreams.

The verse in Galatians came back to life for me that day.

(Do not) become weary in doing good. For at the proper time, you will reap a harvest, if you do not give up. Galatians 6:9 [NIV]

Like the farmer, I planted my seed. Surrendered it to the ground to die, to wait, and to see what the Lord would do with the little I had to offer. This personifies a life of ministry— surrendering the little you have to offer to the One who can do far more with it than you could ever imagine.

Kate Guajardo, a wife and mom of two, has assisted her husband Aaron in youth and young adult ministry for the past eight years. A school teacher, she loves to teach reading and writing. For fun, she enjoys cooking, decorating cakes, and throwing parties for family and friends. Kate and her husband are presently taking on a new position as Dean of Students at Southwestern University in Waxahachie, Texas. Kate grew up as a youth in one of the churches Lee and Sharon pastored.

Chapter 25

Roberta

By Roberta Crabtree

First a minister's daughter; then a minister's wife. I had seen the ugly side of ministry as a teenager. I knew my mother periodically slipped into a corner of our dark, musty basement to pray *and* cry. Dad pastored a clothes-line church, full of "Don't do this." and Don't do that." The congregation spent their energy gripping--showing no compassion for the lost. In spite of this, many young couples started attending, and eventually, this group formed a new congregation which became a thriving church. Years later, remembering that experience, I often reflected on my parents love for the Lord, one another, and those they served. *They were faithful in the good times. They were faithful in the bad times.*

Having been raised in a parsonage gave me a 'heads up' on ministry. I already knew we would never please everyone. I knew there would be moments of rejoicing and times of pain. BUT I also knew *my* personal walk with the Lord, *my* attitude, and how *I* supported my husband would greatly affect our ministry. Still, I had much to learn along the way.

Early in our ministry, I sprawled across the bed one day, crying out to God about the way we were being treated. I thought God would comfort me with loving words, confirming my terrible life. Instead, God firmly told me to adjust *my* attitude. My self-pity hurt me far more than anyone else. He assured me that I could complain to Him, otherwise, I needed to keep my mouth shut.

Some lessons are hard to learn.

Years later we were presented as candidates for a church that suffered in the throes of division and confusion. *We said we were not willing to be considered. God said it was HIS will for us to go there.*

Moses became my Biblical hero for the next eighteen months. He was miraculously called to lead the Israelites—he didn't want the assignment. God warned him it would be tough. God confirmed to us that we were on a difficult journey.

One Sunday a man in the congregation arrived at the church driving a borrowed hearse with a coffin in the back. He and his sons were dressed in black. This gentleman proceeded to stand at the church entrance, informing everyone that my husband, the pastor, was killing the church.

Bob and I sat in our family room that afternoon, hurting so badly that we uttered not one word to each other. We lost two hundred people those eighteen months but God sent four hundred new folks. Some of my most intimate times with the Lord were during those painful months.

Our first step had been to obey the Lord

Our next step was to trust Him.

We left less than four years later when Bob became the

leader for our churches in Ohio. Leaving, however, was not easy because we had learned to love that congregation. I have prayed this little prayer many times:

Lord, help me accept my weaknesses and failures without fear. Help me accept the weaknesses and failures of others without frustration.

Lord, help me accept my strengths and successes without pride and help me accept the strengths and successes of others without intimidation.

Roberta Crabtree *and her husband, Robert, now retired, spent thirteen years in pastoral ministry; eleven years as missionaries; and twenty-one years in state leadership; (Robert as Superintendent of churches in their denomination and Roberta as Director of the Women's Department). She experienced and lived firsthand the life in a pastor's home.*

Sharon Lebsack

Chapter 26

Shannon

By Shannon Veazey

A new command I give you: Love one another. As I have loved you, so you must love one another. John 13:34 [NIV]

Extravagant: Exceeding the bounds of reason. Going beyond what is deserved or justifiable. God's love to us is truly extravagant. God gives His love to us freely, not based on merit and without any compensation.

I've been a pastor's kid my whole life. I loved ministry. I married a wonderful man who is also a pastor's kid and called to ministry. Together we went through our college years, welcomed three children, youth pastored, associate pastored and on to pastor our first church. Those were the years that God grew us and allowed us to see so many things about ministry we only THOUGHT we knew. They were good years-- learning to trust God, value family and to serve wholeheartedly.

God chose to move us to our second pastorate, a larger church with more obligations and issues. For five years we endured some intense opposition from the church board. Suddenly in the matter of one Sunday, a large number of our church members walked away. It was heartbreaking. Our presbyter and our district stood with us. We loved this church and its people and we would stay through this challenging healing process.

An exhausting six months followed: sorting through finances, learning new budgets, building a new facility and working with a new church staff. I felt hurt, stress and bitterness. Some of those who left were supposed to be my friends. I pretended to smile but inside my heart was crushed and my anger began building walls.

One Sunday evening God truly began to deal with me about this anger. I remember weeping and begging for forgiveness. I wanted my heart to be free again. Free to love. Free to let people in. Free to be happy. This night I prayed for **Extravagant Love**--a love that would come from my heart, a love that would not be shaken by circumstances or hurt. I immediately began to feel God's love and a change deep within.

A few weeks later we were sitting in a little café when one of my friends that had left during the church split walked in the door. Without thinking, I ran to her and gave her a big hug. This was REAL! We talked for a few moments and I went back to my seat. I sat there in amazement. What came over me? **Extravagant Love** just happened--a love that exceeds the bounds of reason, a love beyond what was expected.

I've learned many lessons in ministry but the <u>*greatest*</u> is about extravagant love. In ministry, and in life, love can break through any walls of hurt or destruction the enemy may throw at us. To this day our family motto is *Love always wins*. I believe it and I model it every day for my family and my church family. When you love, you are reflecting the heart of God. And His heart is the heart I choose to follow. I want that to always be revealed in my life above everything else.

Shannon Veazey and her husband Gary have been senior pastors at Outreach of Love Church in Springtown, Texas for 20 years. Shannon serves as the Worship/Executive Pastor. Gary and Shannon have been married for 28 years and have 3 children. As a pastor's wife for over 27 years, she has a deep desire to mentor, connect and embrace women in ministry. Shannon is the visionary and leader of "Unveiled "which is a ministry to pastors' wives of the North Texas Assemblies of God.

Sharon Lebsack

Part Seven
Looking Forward

"Many things about tomorrow
I don't seem to understand
But I know who holds tomorrow
And I know who holds my hand." ~Ira Stanphill

Sharon Lebsack

Chapter 27
Sharon's True Confessions

They say that confessions are good for the soul. They're even better when nobody hears them. ~Billy "The Kid" Rosario

Here are the confessions of a pastor's wife. I Confess:

1. I love my husband and family with all of my heart, soul, and being.
2. I love the Father, Son, and Holy Spirit for all they are to my life.
3. I'm a procrastinator in some things. Example: it's taken me 25 years to write this book.
4. I'm passive-aggressive.
5. I love to study people's oddities.
6. I love researching different subjects, places, and things.
7. I've never known exactly who I am.
8. I'm sometimes a Golden Retriever (loving).

9. I'm sometimes a Bolognese (quiet).

10. I'm sometimes a Poodle (faithful, alert, active).

11. I'm sometimes a Dachshund (aggressive).

12. I'm sometimes a Great Dane (protective).

13. I'm sometimes a Springer Spaniel (bouncy, energetic, and fun-loving). Sometimes I talk negatively about myself. (Who do I think I am? Nobody.)

14. I never sought the position of being the wife of a pastor. God did it and I'm glad.

15. My growth times in the Lord often were looked at as defeats—not growths.

16. I was born with a strong desire to encourage and coach others.

17. I fight daily not to be negative, therefore I don't like being around negative people.

18. I'm an obsessive person in projects, exercise, nutrition, cleanliness, and more.

19. I would rather be awake than asleep.

20. I dread, even avoid, confrontations.

21. I do not like to talk on the phone, except with my family. I avoid it whenever possible.

22. If I get down on life, I try to hold and love on a little grand or great-grandchild. In these times, I often call my older grandchildren.

23. I dearly love telling stories of life, especially to my youngest grandchildren.

24. I know I'm not perfect, but I am loved.

25. I know you are loved.

As I reflect back I would not change one thing about being a pastor's wife. BUT GOD KNEW! It took him a long time to convince me that this was His plan and His purpose for me. I have confessed to you, the reader, my many struggles. I found the "pressure times" a blessing in disguise. Hopefully, something of what you read will help you along the way.

God Bless you, my friend.

Sharon Lebsack

ABOUT THE AUTHOR

After over fifty years as a pastor's wife, Sharon Lebsack sees her role in retirement as an encourager and a support to her family and friends. On her God-ordained ministry, she continues to find joy and fulfillment in life.

As an author and speaker, Sharon has been a favorite at conferences, churches, retreats, and seminars for over thirty years. She has touched hearts across America as a TV host with her husband, Lee.

Singing, directing music, teaching God's word, facilitating women's groups, writing curriculum, and working with the women's district ministry, Sharon shares the gifts God has given her. She wrote, produced and starred in a video series on parent/teen relationships. Being a life coach continues into retirement for Sharon as she helps others find their purpose.

Because of Sharon's strong heart for women, she has written

over fifty "Encouraging Words" (an internet based-newsletter), distributed over the world for women—ministers, wives, missionaries, neighbors, friends, and more—for seven years. Today, Sharon Lebsack's ministry to women continues in her writing, Bible studies, and speaking engagements.

If you would like to contact Sharon:

Sharon Lebsack
P.O. Box 7128
Granbury, Texas 76049
sharonkaylebsack@yahoo.com

The bumps in the road aren't as troubling while trusting the Driver—God the Father, Son, and Holy Spirit. ~ Sharon

Made in the USA
Lexington, KY
28 February 2018